DESPERATE DEPENDENCE

Blessings

DESPERATE DEPENDENCE

EXPERIENCING GOD'S BEST
IN LIFE'S TOUGHEST SITUATIONS

by
Max Davis

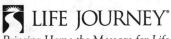

LIFE JOURNEY
Bringing Home the Message for Life

An Imprint of Cook Communications Ministries
COLORADO SPRINGS, COLORADO • PARIS, ONTARIO
KINGSWAY COMMUNICATIONS, LTD., EASTBOURNE, ENGLAND

Life Journey® is an imprint of
Cook Communications Ministries, Colorado Springs, CO 80918
Cook Communications, Paris, Ontario
Kingsway Communications, Eastbourne, England

DESPERATE DEPENDENCE
© 2004 by Max Davis

**Published in association with the literary agency of Mark Gilroy
Communications, Inc., 6528 East 101st Street, Tulsa, OK 74133-6754.**

Cover Design: Ray Moore/Two Moore Designs
Cover Photo: © JP Sruchet / Getty Images

First Printing, 2004
Printed in the United States of America
1 2 3 4 5 6 7 8 9 10 Printing/Year 08 07 06 05 04

Unless otherwise noted, Scripture quotations are taken from the *Holy Bible:
New International Version*®. Copyright © 1973, 1978, 1984 by
International Bible Society. Used by permission of Zondervan Publishing
House. All rights reserved. Verses marked TLB are taken from *The Living
Bible*, © 1971, Tyndale House Publishers, Wheaton, IL 60189. Used by
permission. Scriptures marked NKJV taken from the *New King James Version*.
Copyright © 1979, 1980, 1982 by Thomas Nelson, Inc. Used by permis-
sion. All rights reserved. Scriptures marked AMP are taken from the
Amplified® Bible, copyright© 1954, 1958, 1962, 1965, 1987 by the
Lockman Foundation. Used by permission.

Library of Congress Cataloging-in-Publication Data

Davis, Max.
  Desperate dependence : experiencing God's best in life's toughest
situations / by Max Davis.
      p. cm.
Includes bibliographical references.
  ISBN 0-7814-4064-5 (pbk.)
  1. Consolation. 2. Trust in God. 3. Suffering--Religious
aspects--Christianity. I. Title.
BV4909.D355 2004
248.8'6--dc22
                                        2003027070

To my parents,
James & Nell Davis

You continue to come through for me in very real
ways and exemplify characteristics that I strive to
emulate in my own life. I love you.

CONTENTS

Acknowledgments

Tasks such as this cannot be completed without the help of many selfless people. Writing a book is truly a community project. First, I would like to thank all those who made time in their busy schedules to share their experiences with me. You are true warriors of the faith and an encouragement to many.

As always, I must thank my wonderful wife, Alanna, for her constant support, encouragement, criticism, and input without which I would not have this career. And to my special mother-in-law, Sharon, for all those times you stopped what you were doing to read my stuff and tell me just what I needed to hear.

Thanks to my agent, Mark Gilroy, for your belief in my writing ability and your constant availability. To Terry Whalin, Linda Vixie, and Mary McNeil and the rest of the Cook family for your support and patience and for making me a better writer. Finally, I would like to thank Terry Dorian for speaking up on my behalf. Blessings to you all.

Author's Note

In the first chapter of this book I talk about going through a painful divorce and separation from my children over twelve years ago. I was the pastor of a growing church and came home one day after service to find myself alone. Shaken to the core, I hit rock bottom—emotionally, spiritually, and financially. In my first two books, *Never Stick Your Tongue Out at Mama and Other Life-Transforming Revelations* and *It's Only a Flat Tire in the Rain*, I wrote in detail about the experience. However, I don't intend to continually revisit that time in my life. God has given me a wonderful wife of ten years, restored my children to me, and blessed my writing career.

I've come to believe deeply in Romans 8:28: "And we know that in all things God works for the good of those who love him, who have been called according to his purpose." I've also come to realize that in this Scripture the words "all things" really mean all things. I'm briefly revisiting that time in my life in this book because it was during that experience that I began to learn what it means to truly live in *desperate dependence* on God.

Foreword

You don't have to live long to know that life is challenging under the best of circumstances and downright overwhelming at times. You are either coming out of a storm or you are right in the middle of a storm or you are just about to go into a storm. It doesn't matter whether you are a believer or not; the storms will come. It doesn't matter whether you have great faith or no faith at all; the storms will come. As Jesus said, "In this world you will have trouble" (John 16:33).

That's why Max Davis's book, *Desperate Dependence*, is so timely. Not only does he write about suffering and sorrow with painful honesty, but he also affirms the truly supernatural sufficiency of God's grace. Or as he says, "Desperate dependence is about experiencing God's best in life's toughest situations."

Max writes with a refreshing honesty that is often lacking in contemporary works. He refuses to gloss over the tough times or to provide easy answers. Instead he tells it like it is with heartbreaking reality and a faith that has been hammered out on the hard anvil of life. The result is a book that is both poignant and inspiring.

Drawing on his own life experience and the experiences of others, as well as the eternal truth of Scripture, Max sheds light—God's light—on life's darkest moments. Again and again he shows us how God takes life's most devastating tragedies and turns them into instruments of His grace. That which the enemy intended for our destruction becomes the very stuff God uses to make us into the men and women He has called us to be.

The reason Max's writing resonates with reality is because he is writing out of his own life experience. He's lived both the heartbreak of personal tragedy and the wonder of God's renewing grace.

Do you struggle with feelings of helplessness and despair as you suffer with your handicapped child? So has Max. His son was born deaf.

Are you haunted by past failures? Do you wonder if you can ever overcome the things that have happened to you? Sometimes Max feels that way too. As a young pastor he suffered a painful divorce and the loss of his church.

Are you struggling to start over, to rebuild your life? Are you weighted down with financial obligations that seem overwhelming? Are you battling to regain your health? Are you trying to learn to live without a departed loved one? If you are, then *Desperate Dependence* is for you. Based on the lessons he's learned, Max teaches us how to make peace with our pain, how to turn it into an ally instead of an enemy.

Faced with life's inevitable tragedies we have three choices. We can curse life for doing this to us and look for some way to express our grief and rage. Or we can grit our teeth and endure it. Or we can accept it. The first alternative is useless. The second is sterile and exhausting. The third is the only way.

Acceptance. Now that's what *Desperate Dependence* is all about. Not resignation, which gives up and says, "Whatever will be will be." But acceptance, which believes for a miracle even as it accepts the reality of present difficulty. Acceptance does not demand a predetermined conclusion; rather it leaves the nature of the miracle to the wisdom of God. It may come in the form of divine intervention in the circumstances of life. Or it may come as a miracle in our spirit, enabling us to experience peace and fulfillment while living in the most desperate straits.

Acceptance means we stop fighting God; we stop blaming Him for life's hardships. It means we stop working against His purposes in our life. Instead, we yield ourselves to Him, we work with Him. And, as a result we experience His supernatural peace.

That's the real strength of Christianity. Not that it makes us immune to life's difficulties, but that it gives us grace to deal with them redemptively. It enables us to be loving in the most hostile relationships, to find joy where others find only futility, and to experience peace even in the time of trouble. That's *Desperate Dependence—Experiencing God's Best in Life's Toughest Situations.*

—Richard Exley, author and speaker

CHAPTER ONE

DESPERATE DEPENDENCE

> "Crises bring us face-to-face with our inadequacy
> and our inadequacy in turn leads us to the
> inexhaustible sufficiency of God."
> —*Catherine Marshall*

*W*ind, whipped in an intense fury, pushed the water into massive waves that swirled and sucked and smashed down upon the man who was fighting for his life. Raindrops slashed across his face, and he gulped large amounts of water as he kicked and gasped in his frantic struggle against nature's cruel turbulence—but to no avail. The man was drowning. And to think, mere moments ago, he was full of courage, stepping out in faith, following his Master's call—but that was then.

Circumstances had abruptly changed, and his confidence had vanished. The sea, along with his fear, was engulfing him, dragging him down deeper into despair. Maybe he had misunderstood. Yet he was almost certain he had heard his Master say, "Come." Yes, he was positive. Surely the Master could be trusted? Surely He wouldn't call him out of the boat only to let him drown? He had never let him down in the past.

"Do something!" the man cried inwardly. "Don't just watch me drown! Do something!"

Then, with one final surge of energy—one last leap of faith—the man lurched up in a desperate attempt to grasp the arm that was reaching down for him. If he could but cling to his Master's hand, the man knew he would be safe.

Shaken to the Core

What if I were the follower of Jesus who had stepped over the edge of that boat into the waves? The man who had turned his eyes from the Master to the maelstrom around me? The above account is how I imagine the scene as Peter stepped out of the boat and attempted to walk on the waves. I took some liberties and read between the lines, but the Scriptures are much more to the point. Read them along with me:

> The boat was already a considerable distance from land, buffeted by the waves because the wind was against it.
>
> During the fourth watch of the night Jesus went out to them, walking on the lake. When the disciples saw him walking on the lake, they were terrified. "It's

a ghost," they said, and cried out in fear.

But Jesus immediately said to them: "Take courage! It is I. Don't be afraid."

"Lord, if it's you," Peter replied, "tell me to come to you on the water."

"Come," he said.

Then Peter got down out of the boat, walked on the water and came toward Jesus. But when he saw the wind, he was afraid and, beginning to sink, cried out, "Lord, save me!"

Immediately Jesus reached out his hand and caught him. (Matt. 14:24–31)

Did you know that the way Peter clung to Christ when he was in fear of drowning is the same way God wants us to live our everyday lives—in desperate dependence upon Him—clinging to Him, knowing full well that if we let go of Him or He lets go of us, we are doomed, without hope, and will surely drown in the sea of our own circumstances and failures? When we live in desperate dependence on Christ, terrified to let go of His hand because we know the minute we try to do the Christian life on our own we will surely fail, then like Peter, we too will walk on the waves of life. God may not make our storms disappear. Sometimes they may intensify. Yet Christ is calling for each of us to come and walk with Him on the sea. We could never do it by our own efforts, for the task is much bigger than we are.

Often at speaking engagements and during interviews I tell people that "losing everything and hitting rock bottom over a decade ago was the best thing that ever happened to me." And I do mean hitting rock bottom. Usually when I make such a statement I get more than a few raised eyebrows. I mean, how can losing everything and hitting rock bottom possibly be the best thing that happened to me? Especially when I had been successful at nearly everything I had attempted—I had attended college on a full athletic scholarship, finished my undergraduate degree on the dean's list, completed my master's degree, pastored a growing church, and had a beautiful home and family—only to end up divorced, separated from my children—one of whom is totally deaf—out of my career, living in a twelve-year-old car, humiliated, hurt, and broken. And I must add that it happened completely out of my control, while I was trying my hardest to do "all the right things."

Of course, it is only fair to acknowledge that out of my own ignorance I had made a plethora of mistakes and bad choices. But how could anyone in his right mind possibly say that losing it all was the best thing that ever happened to him? I can say it because it wasn't until I was broken—financially, emotionally, and spiritually—that I was forced out of my safe zone and began clinging in desperate dependence to God.

Ever since becoming a Christian in high school and all through college, graduate school, and during my time as a pastor, my beliefs about God were nice and clean, all laid out straight and orderly in my neat little psychological box. What I believed was comfortable. It fit me. If someone asked me why I believed what I did, I'd reply with something to the tune of "Well, the Bible is God's Word and if God said it, then

I believe it!" All that is fine and dandy, but I didn't really know why I believed it, just that I was supposed to. And because what I believed was never really challenged, I was fine going through the motions of my Christianity. But when my life was shaken to the core and everything I held dear came crashing down, my neat little box was tipped over, and all my comfortable beliefs came spilling out. For over two years I was like a little kid scrambling on the floor after spilled crayons, trying frantically to find something—some unbroken belief—to put back in my box.

Then, over time, I sensed a beautiful pattern emerging. Day by day, month by month, I was becoming acutely aware that in this process of searching and scratching urgently for answers, I was not just talking to God, but I was crying out for Him, pleading for His truth and for His provision. I was at the point of utter brokenness and humility, desperate for Him. A death was taking place—the death of me. As Brennan Manning said in *The Ragamuffin Gospel*, I was "impossible to insult." Nothing was left to insult. I had nothing to be proud of, yet my inner poverty of spirit was setting me free. I knew I was weak and that only God could drag me out of my pit. Helpless, I was now truly looking to God as my source. As a result, God was showing Himself real to me as never before, both spiritually and practically.

I remember vividly the first week I slept in my car, unable to find a job. I was literally penniless and famished. I'm sure I could have called my father and mother, who lived four states away, but my pride kept me from doing that. I'll spare you the unpleasant details that landed me in the situation, but I was poorer than I had ever been in my life and I was hungry. So I got out of my car and began walking down the sidewalk.

Walking, I silently cried out to God in desperation. "God," I pleaded, "I know You are real and alive. I've based my whole life on the fact of Your realness and Your ever-present, ever-caring nature. Please, God! Provide for me. Make a way where there seems to be no way. Please, I'm coming to You because Your Word tells me to."

Over and over, I quoted the promises of God. As I prayed and walked, recalling the Word of God, I looked down toward my feet and, I kid you not, there was a twenty-dollar bill stuck in the gutter! The food that day never tasted better.

Here's where the story gets really wild. A couple of days later, I was again broke and hungry and was walking down the same street praying the same prayer. I said to God, "If You did it once, I know You can do it again." As I walked and prayed, I looked down and there was a ten-dollar bill lying on the sidewalk! Tell me, when was the last time you found a twenty just lying on a sidewalk, or a ten, or both, in just a couple of days?

God was indeed real. In the midst of my pain and questions, He knew exactly where I was. Since that time, until this day, God has never failed me. He called me to step out in faith and start a writing and publishing career with no money, enormous debt, and a busted ego, when nearly everyone thought I was crazy. But God has miraculously provided every step of the way. He has opened doors that absolutely no human could open. Most of all, though, He's given me my life back along with a wonderful wife who is my best friend, a new daughter, and both of my children from my previous marriage who live with us and love God. Things haven't always been perfect. There have been issues to work through, especially as a blended family, but God has most definitely been faithful.

Please understand that I do not believe for a second that divorce, separation from your children, and losing your finances are God's doing. But I do know that coming to the point of desperate dependence was exactly where God wanted me. He knew all that was going to happen and used it for my growth. Looking back, I now actually praise God for those broken years because out of them came a faith stronger and more sure than I could have ever imagined.

Getting Out of the Zone

Previously, I mentioned the "safe zone." Your safe zone is that place in life where you are not really fulfilled or experiencing God's best, yet life is too comfortable and safe to do anything different. Deep down you long for something you can't quite put your finger on. You sense that more is out there for you, but fear of change, fear of failure, or fear of what others may think has you chained in the prison of false security. So sometimes, as an act of grace, God will use painful and unpleasant circumstances to force us out of our safe zone. That's what happened to me. It wasn't by choice.

Unlike the safe zone, however, desperate dependence is that place where God *truly* becomes your source. I emphasize the word *truly* because so often we say or think we are depending on God when in reality we are depending on everything but God. I mean, let's get real here. Most of us base our self-worth on how other people view us and respond to us. But what happens when someone doesn't like us or disagrees with us or misunderstands us?

Often we depend on our own works and performance for righteous standing with God. But what happens when we fail repeatedly and lose confidence in our own ability? We depend on companies and institutions for our incomes, but what happens when economies go bust and we lose our jobs? We are dependent on our careers, accomplishments, and relationships for fulfillment, but what happens when we burn out or the dynamic feelings fade? We depend on circumstances for our happiness, but what happens when circumstances change, out of our control? What happens when the columns on which we rest our hopes and securities are knocked out from under us and we are left with nothing but God to cling to? Is God enough? Can God be trusted to provide for our needs, both practical and spiritual? Luke 12:28 (NKJV) says, "If then God so clothes the grass, which today is in the field and tomorrow is thrown into the oven, how much more will He clothe you?"

Are Scriptures like these really relevant for our high-tech society? Are God and this thing called Christianity for real, to the point of laying our lives and reputations on the line, or have we all been duped into playing some sort of psychological game? In order to experience the fullness of the Christian life we must be able to answer those questions, and it's at the point of desperate dependence that we find the answer to be a fervent yes! The bottom line is this: coming to the point of desperate dependence is coming to the end of ourselves. And it's at that point God begins His greatest work in us. It's where miracles happen and we enter into a deeper, more intimate walk with God than we ever thought possible. It's the point where we can experience God's best in life's toughest situations.

Frequently I'm asked, "Are you saying we have to hit rock bottom to experience God's best?" No. We don't all have to hit rock bottom as I did, but we most definitely must come to the point of desperate dependence and unfortunately, most of us need a little help getting there. In every season of our lives, on each level, God is calling us to desperately depend on Him. God wants us to depend on Him in times of prosperity and comfort as well as in times of crisis. The eminent theologian John Calvin said, "Trusting God allows for gratitude in prosperity and patience in adversity."

Personally, God is still giving me new and fresh opportunities in which to desperately depend on Him. Having a deaf son has greatly challenged my faith. Almost constantly I feel inadequate as a father and am learning to daily place my son in God's care. Let me tell you, nothing hurts like seeing your child hurt. Being a father of two girls has its own challenges. Each day I'm seeing that if I'm not depending on God, I can't hope to be the husband my wife needs me to be. My career is exciting, but in it I must trust God for His provision. As a result, the book you are reading is my third!

And most importantly, I'm coming to realize that my relationship with Christ is not based on my performance, but upon His provision at the Cross—grace, not just for salvation, but for my daily walk as well. The only righteousness that matters is the righteousness that comes from trusting Him. I'm living what C. S. Lewis wrote about in *Mere Christianity*: *"Our failures and life's buffeting* cures our illusions about ourselves and teaches us to depend on God. We learn, on the one hand, that we cannot trust ourselves even in our best moments and, on the other, that we need not despair even in our worst, for our failures are forgiven. The only fatal thing is to sit down content with anything less than perfection" (emphasis added).[1]

God Meant It for Good

The theme of desperate dependence is nothing new. God has forever been leading His servants to the end of themselves before He uses them in mighty ways.

Moses was strong, well-educated, good-looking, and passionate for the things of God, but God couldn't use him until he had come to the end of himself. I'm sure that on more than a few occasions Moses thought, "All my talents and abilities are just going to waste out here in the desert." Yet God knew exactly where Moses was, and after he spent forty years in the desert as a shepherd, when his speaking ability and influence were gone, then God said it was time. Moses went out, but he clung to God in desperate dependence as he went.

What about Joseph? Scholars say he spent about fifteen years as a slave and prisoner before God moved him out. Can you imagine being disowned by your family and then going to prison for a crime you didn't commit? And not for a few months or even a year, but for fifteen years! Joseph was well-acquainted with injustice. However, he remained faithful and chose to trust God in his circumstances when nothing appeared to make sense. When God finally did intervene, Joseph went from being a prisoner to second in charge of a nation in a matter of hours! Afterward, he was able to say with confidence and compassion to his brothers, "But as for you, you meant evil against me; but God meant it for good" (Gen. 50:20 NKJV).

As God led Moses and the children of Israel out of Egypt, with Pharaoh's army nipping at their heels, where did God lead them? Right up against the Red Sea—a place where only He could deliver them. Talk about desperate dependence! They knew that if God didn't come through for them, they would be dead meat.

God pitted a young shepherd boy named David against the top military giant in the land. He waited until Abraham and Sarah were too old to have kids—then gave them Isaac. God told Gideon his army was too big, to reduce its size so they would depend on Him and not themselves. And so the stories go throughout the entire Bible: God bringing His people to the place of desperate dependence so He can reveal Himself to them.

Be of Good Cheer

Obviously, no one ever wishes for pain and adversity to visit his or her life. We don't volunteer to lose a job or a home. It's not a life goal to experience the collapse of a cherished relationship or to watch a child suffer. We don't plan on losing our health. But, my friend, if you haven't realized it by now, struggle and tribulation are inevitable. They are going to happen and that's not a morbid statement. It's simply a fact of living in this fallen world. Jesus Himself said in John 16:33 (NKJV), "In the world you *will* have tribulation" (emphasis added).

Webster defines tribulation as misfortune, trials, suffering, pain, distress, trouble, and problems. Jesus wasn't being a pessimist. He was being a realist. Adversity is going to happen. Each time it does, however, regardless of its depth and level of pain, we have a unique opportunity to desperately depend on God and allow Him to take us to a deeper level and use us in remarkable ways as only He can. Yes, we will have tribulation, but we are not to be fearful. Jesus said in the same verse, "Be of good cheer, I have overcome the world."

When you consider Jesus' words here, they are short, sweet, and powerful. I ask you, though, is it realistic to "be of good cheer" when in deep pain? I mean, just today, for example, a friend asked me to pray for him and his son. His thirty-six-year-old son has terminal colon cancer. Are they supposed to "be of good cheer"? It sounds to me as if Jesus was being a little idealistic.

Yet the cheer Jesus was talking about is not some bubbly, giddy feeling that stems from a person's happiness or up-and-down emotional state. It is not positive confession. This cheer is not the absence of pain, but rather a deep-seated peace and joy that settles the heart of a believer in the midst of the most adverse circumstances. This type of peace and joy allows one to experience pain with full emotion, yet not as someone without hope. It's a confidence that says, "I feel the pain. I know the risks. I see my inadequacies, but I'm moving forward in faith—clinging in desperate dependence to my God."

Standing up to the Test

Johnny Nicosia is one of the most Christlike men you could ever meet. He is one of those people who when you walk away from even a short encounter with him you are changed. When talking with him you would think his life is full of wonder and happiness, but it's not. Johnny has battled a severe form of brain cancer for over five years. On several occasions, doctors gave him only weeks to live. Yet he is not bitter at life; instead he is experiencing God's best in one of life's toughest situations.

Johnny told me that he handled the news of having brain cancer and dying much better than having brain cancer and the possibility of having to live with it. His desperate dependence on God began on what started out to be a routine day on October 7, 1998. By day's end, however, it wasn't so routine because he found himself in the hospital emergency room recovering from a massive seizure and being scheduled for immediate brain surgery.

Until that point his life was pretty normal and good. His marriage was strong, and he had three beautiful, healthy children. Johnny had never really had any earth-shattering events confront him. Both he and his wife, Robyn, were thankful and had little to complain about. But deep in their spirits they longed for something more—to know Christ in a deeper, more intimate way. Day after day Johnny and Robyn asked

God to use them in a special way. Johnny told me that he "personally had felt like Job before his test—that a hedge was around me and my faith had never really been tested. Because of this, there was one main question that kept continually nagging me. How do I know if my relationship with God will stand up to a test?" That is what his heart was yearning to know. Did God not trust him enough to test him? Did God know he would fail? Did God think he would fall away? Was Johnny not spiritually mature enough to go through the fire? These questions festered deep inside him.

When the fiery trial of cancer began, it did not take Johnny long to admit that he had never considered developing brain cancer an answer to prayer! Though Johnny knew that God did not give him cancer, he did know that for some reason God had allowed it. "God's peace, the peace that passes all understanding, sustained me to the point that the thought of dying didn't bother me at all," Johnny said. "I was ready to depart and be with the Lord."

But, as always, God's ways are higher than our ways, and God has seen fit to keep Johnny here to testify to His faithfulness. In fact, it was the living with cancer that would prove to be the real test. For five years he has received chemotherapy treatments that have weakened and changed his body. Then there's been the financial pressure that comes with this disease. Things haven't been easy. Some days, Johnny admits, he has wished the Lord would just take him home. Yet he knows Robyn and the kids need him. But God has been faithful and has met them at every stage. Johnny's body continues to bounce back with unusual strength. The treatments have worked! God's healing power is real. On several occasions the doctors had written him off, but God hasn't written him off.

Financially, God has always made a way. The body of Christ, their family, and friends at work all rallied, helping to lift the financial burden. "We have been blown away by the way God's people have responded to our need, when we never asked for anything!" Johnny said.

Perhaps the following words are the most important thing Johnny said. They are both profound and challenging. "This whole process has been life-changing for me. *I know now that God loved me too much to leave me as I was. He is using this process to help change my wife and me more and more into His image.*"

What powerful words of encouragement! God loved Johnny too much to leave him as he was. I know you may say, "Come on, now, you don't really expect me to believe that?" But it's true. I know it sounds crazy, but Johnny and Robyn really do praise God for this experience! Not only has it brought them closer to the Lord, but it has brought them closer together as a couple. Their love has experienced new depths since this trial began.

I too have experienced what Johnny and Robyn have. Though I would not want to experience the pain of divorce again and though I do not enjoy the anguish I feel for my deaf son, I wouldn't take a million dollars for what I've learned.

When going through my own ordeal, at times the emotional pain was so excruciating that sometimes I would ball up in a corner and just weep. Once, while traveling at night, the pain was so great that I literally couldn't drive. I pulled my car onto the shoulder of the road, got out, and paced up and down the interstate crying out to God until the pain subsided somewhat and I was able to get back in the car and move on. That's how I survived.

During that time, my relationship with God consisted of my crying out, "God! Help!" I wasn't saying all the right things, believing all the right things, or doing all the right things. I couldn't set foot in a church for a long time. It was too painful. The only thing—I mean, the only thing—that sustained me during that time was clinging to Jesus. Sometimes my faith wavered. I had many hard questions, but I clung to God and He brought me through. Often clinging isn't pretty or pious; it's simply desperate.

> "Immediately Jesus reached out his
> hand and caught him."
> —*Matthew 14:31*

CHAPTER TWO

RECOGNIZING CHRIST IN THE STORM

"Those who navigate little streams and shallow creeks, know but little of the God of tempests; but those who 'do business in great waters,' these see His 'wonders in the deep.' Among the huge Atlantic waves of bereavement, poverty, temptation, and reproach, we learn the power of Jehovah, because we feel the littleness of man."
—*Charles Spurgeon*

*L*et's get back to the disciples' boat being knocked around by the wind and waves and Jesus rescuing them. What's interesting about this story is that it was Jesus Himself who sent the disciples into the tempest. Christ's followers were walking in full obedience. They were obeying God. Scriptures declare plainly that "Jesus made the disciples get into the boat and go on ahead of him to the other side, while he dismissed the crowd. After he had dismissed them, he went up on a mountainside by himself to pray" (Matt. 14:22–23).

As the disciples, out of sheer obedience, climbed into the boat and launched into the sea, some undoubtedly wondered why. The move probably didn't make much sense to them. How was Jesus going to walk and meet them? It would take Him a long time to walk around the sea and meet them on the other side—possibly a couple of days. Obviously, if Jesus were going to meet them anytime soon, He would have to hitch a ride on another boat. Why couldn't He just ride with them as He had always done? They could wait until He dismissed the crowd. They could hang out while He went up the mountain to pray. Nevertheless, despite their questions, they did what Jesus said. They were doing the "right thing." They were obeying the Lord. Yet after following in faith, they found themselves fighting for their lives during a raging storm.

Present in the Storm

Somewhere along the path of life, many of us have picked up the notion that if we are experiencing storms then we must be out of the will of God—that smooth sailing, blessing, and prosperity are God's stamp of approval, and if things get rough, well, we must be doing something wrong. Yes, adversity often is a direct result of our sin and mistakes. Sometimes we just mess up or someone else messes up and it affects us. When that happens we need to acknowledge our mistake, repent, and make the appropriate adjustments. Sometimes, however, we can be right in the center of God's will and still experience the most violent storms of our lives.

Think about this. While the disciples were losing their fight against the elements, Jesus was on top of a mountain praying. The mountain overlooked the sea. Jesus was probably watching them the whole time. He was well aware of the storm and how they were struggling. Then, in His perfect timing, when despair overtook them, Jesus showed up in the middle of the storm, something they'd never considered. I like how the *Amplified Bible* describes what Jesus told His disciples after He strolled out to them and they mistook him for a ghost. "But instantly He spoke to them, saying, Take courage! I AM! Stop being afraid!" (Matt. 14:27).

Jesus was telling them, "Hey, guys. I'm God! I'm the Maker of the universe. I made this lake. This storm is no big deal for Me. I can handle it. If I am for you, who can be against you?"

You see, up to that point, they had seen Jesus do miracles. In fact, they had just watched Him feed five thousand people with two fish and five small loaves of bread. They had heard His words of life, seen Him cast out demons and set captives free, but they hadn't learned to trust Him in the midst of the storm. Where have we heard that before? Sounds a lot like "In the world you will have tribulation; but be of good cheer, I have overcome the world" (John 16:33 NKJV).

The important thing for us to remember is that in their bleakest, darkest moment, when it seemed certain that the small boat was going to capsize and lose its battle with the elements, Jesus met them there. This tells me that Jesus was watching them, waiting for the right moment. The disciples had never left His mind. Jesus wanted them to learn to trust Him. He wasn't being cruel but was teaching them a valuable lesson, a lesson that He wants to teach us. He is present in our storms. Jesus understood that the disciples could never fully know Him or trust Him until they experienced the full rage of the storm and then saw Him in the tempest with them. Jesus wanted them to learn how to be of good cheer, even when the boat appeared to be sinking. Jesus wants us to be of good cheer even when it appears our boat is sinking, when circumstances look hopeless, when there seems to be no way out.

When the disciples finally did see Jesus, they didn't even recognize Him and thought He was a ghost. To be fair, what would you think if you saw a man walking on the water in the middle of the night, in a raging storm? The fact that they thought Jesus was a ghost tells me something. It tells me their mind-set. They were so wrapped up in their fight for survival that it never occurred to them that Jesus was present with them and aware of what they were going through. How often are we too absorbed in our own pain and turmoil to recognize God? Yet He is there waiting.

In Daniel 3:16–30 we see three Hebrew young men, Shadrach, Meshach, and Abednego, about to be executed by being tossed into a blazing furnace. But what happened when King Nebuchadnezzar checked out the situation? He exclaimed, "Weren't there three men that we tied up and threw into the fire?…[Yet] I see four men walking around in the fire, unbound and unharmed, and the fourth looks like a son of the gods!"(vv. 24–25).

As He was for the disciples in their storm and the three Hebrews in the fire, Jesus is present in our tribulations. God wants us to know Him as Jehovah-Shalom—the God that gives peace in the midst of trouble (Judges 6) and as Jehovah-Sammah—the God who is with you always (Ezekiel 48). And He wants us to know that our troubles have a purpose. They are to bring us to complete rest and trust in His power and presence at all times.

It's not hard, however, to lose the sense of His presence when we are in painful and desperate situations. More than often, we feel abandoned, left to struggle against bleak odds. As C. S. Lewis said in *A Grief Observed*, we cry out to God only to hear "a door slammed in [our] face, and a sound of bolting and double bolting on the inside. After that, silence."[2] Sometimes it feels as if we're all alone in that tossing boat, battered by massive waves and powerful winds, but we are not. Jesus wants us to know that He is there with us.

A Blanket of Peace

In the late 1970s, Norman Williams was aboard a 747 jet when it collided on the runway with another 747. Five hundred eighty-one passengers and crew lost their lives, making it the worst air disaster in history at that time. Miraculously, Williams survived to tell his story—a vivid illustration of Jesus' presence in the storm. Listen to his words:

I have had some marvelous spiritual experiences throughout my life. But I have never sensed the presence of the Holy Spirit as I did in that indescribable fury. The Spirit of God was so strong. It was as if a blanket of peace was thrown over me—I wasn't numb—a lucid calm enveloped me. I was in the midst of a fiery bomb yet I knew all was well. I did not move in panic. I did not move in fear. I did not even move as if my life depended on it. That wasn't me—no one can act that way. I knew it was beyond man—any man.

You might say I did not move at all, but that I was moved. The Spirit of God moving, directing me. My head ducked a piece of white-hot debris hurtling at one hundred miles per hour—enough to decapitate me. Somehow my head darted just in time as it whistled past. I shouted, "I stand upon Your Word! I stand upon Your Word!" Each time I proclaimed those words new hope and new strength surged in me. Here in the midst of the worst human tragedy I could imagine was the greatest spiritual experience I could dream of.

What does one do trapped in a cauldron of death? Get out the 747 brochure and check out the exits? Listen to the moans of anguish? Call information? You are so alone. How about help from a stewardess? The purser? The captain himself? They're all busy living or dying. You have to go higher. The President of the United States? Higher, still.

In the moment of reckoning, you do have a friend in a high place. Just one. He is never too busy or out to lunch. He will make house calls, anywhere…. He came to me….A flow of life through me was being expressed in feeling, *a feeling of God's presence.* I know I am watched over by God, taken care of by God. I am nobody special, yet somebody special to Him.[3]

Like Norman Williams and the disciples in that boat, regardless of your storm, Jesus is there. Look for Him and you will find Him.

> "And surely I am with you always,
> to the very end of the age."
> —*Jesus (Matt. 28:20)*

CHAPTER THREE

A FAITH THAT PLEASES

> "Faith is being certain of something you can't see—
> being keenly aware of the unseen divine realities all
> around you."
> —*Joni Eareckson Tada*

The eleventh chapter of Hebrews is the famous faith chapter. In it we are told what faith is and then given a list of men and women who were great in faith. We are told about Noah who, in faith, obeyed God and was supernaturally delivered from the Flood, and about Sarah who received the miracle baby, Isaac, though she was much too old.

Hebrews goes on to say that they "through faith subdued kingdoms, worked righteousness, obtained promises, stopped the mouths of lions, quenched the violence of fire, escaped the edge of the sword, out of weakness were made strong, became valiant in battle, turned to flight the armies of the aliens. Women received their dead raised to life again" (Heb. 11:33–35 NKJV).

This is pretty awesome stuff, right? God is a God of miracles! I can do all things through Christ! We have the victory! If God is for us, who can be against us? Now, let's get out there and move that mountain! Rah! Rah! But before we launch our attack, we should read further. "Still others had trial of mockings and scourgings, yes, and of chains and imprisonment. They were stoned, they were sawn in two, were tempted, were slain with the sword. They wandered about in sheepskins and goatskins, being destitute, afflicted, tormented" (vv. 36–37 NKJV).

What? Sawn in two? Slain with the sword? Tormented and destitute? Afflicted? I can handle the obtaining promises part or stopping the mouths of lions, but I don't know about this destitute and afflicted stuff.

Isn't that just like us? We're always quick to give God praise when something positive comes into our lives, but when uncomfortable or painful things that have come our way do not instantly disappear, we are just as quick to shake our finger at the sky, questioning God's goodness.

God's Silence

For a moment, let's step back in time. Picture this poor fellow who has served God faithfully and now is about to be sawn in half. I can't even begin to imagine the agony he must have been going through. No doubt he had a wife and children who were left behind. Who knows, they might have witnessed the whole thing. Public executions were common back then, with the crowd most likely hurling insults. It was not a pretty sight.

Being sawn in two was a long, excruciating death. The saw did not cut like a sharp knife or chop like a guillotine. It actually tore or ripped the skin and tissue little by little. It's enough to make you want to scream, "God, where are You? Why are You allowing this? Can't You do something? Surely a loving God would put a stop to this!"

Why is it that God delivered so many, yet not this one? Why was God silent? If the man would have had more faith could he have been delivered? Perhaps he wasn't positive enough or confessing the right words? Not a chance. This guy is listed right there beside all the others who had great faith. Did you get that? This wonderful man of God did not see a divine intervention to his problem, but according to God, he had as much faith as anyone.

So what is God trying to tell us here? Why did He end such a positive chapter on such a sour note? I mean, you never hear people quoting to themselves, "They were…destitute, afflicted, tormented…and…having obtained a good testimony through faith, did not receive the promise" (Heb. 11:37–39 NKJV).

Those are Scriptures we just don't want to hear. Could it be that there are two sides of this faith walk? There's the one side that finds itself totally and helplessly thrown upon God in desperate need of supernatural deliverance. And then there's the other side of faith that calls upon God for divine strength, peace, and courage to go through any situation that is handed to us. The side of faith we get to use depends on God, not us. We simply need to be in a position to receive the grace God gives us, whatever form it takes.

Bible commentator F. F. Bruce said about this passage:

Some through faith, we have been told, "escaped the edge of the sword," but some through faith, "were slain with the sword." ... By faith one lived, and by faith the other died. ... Faith in God carries with it no guarantee of comfort in this world: this was no doubt one of the lessons which our author wished his readers to learn.[4]

Have you ever considered what happened to John the Baptist? After preparing the way for Jesus, baptizing Him, and seeing the Holy Spirit descend upon Him, John wound up in prison about to be beheaded. Stuck in that cold, dark jail cell, facing execution, the man of God began to have some doubts. So John sent a messenger to ask Jesus if He was really the Christ. Jesus responded to the messenger, "Go back and report to John what you hear and see: The blind receive sight, the lame walk, those who have leprosy are cured, the deaf hear, the dead are raised, and the good news is preached to the poor. Blessed is the man who does not fall away on account of me" (Matt. 11:4–6).

What is interesting here is that Jesus did not rescue John the Baptist from prison. Nor did He show the least bit of concern for his welfare. In fact, Jesus' response to John's question seems rather cold. You'll notice that Jesus didn't even go visit John. I'm quite certain that John the Baptist felt the silence of God and wondered why. And John never did get rescued and eventually was beheaded! This leaves us wondering why Jesus would let John lose his head, but raise Lazarus and several others from the dead. Did Jesus love Lazarus more? Was John the Baptist lacking in faith? I don't think so. In Matthew 11:11 Jesus said of John the Baptist, "I tell you the truth: Among those born of women there has not risen anyone greater than John the Baptist."

Sometimes God does not rescue us and, as with John the Baptist or Job, He gives us no reason.

I love the Bible's honesty. The fact that the Bible is so honest has been a great source of comfort to me. People consistently ask, "If God is so good then why…?" But as we saw in chapter 1, Jesus said, "In the world you will have tribulation." In His Word, God never even remotely hints that this life will always be easy, and He does not hide the fact that people of faith, like John the Baptist and the guy sawn in two, may go through tough times. What He does say, over and over, is that He will be there in the storm with us. But we have to make the choice to believe or not. The great sin of the world is not adultery or stealing or lying or homosexuality or murder. The great sin of the world is unbelief—not trusting in God's goodness.

Faith pleases God. Hebrews 11:6 says, "Without faith it is impossible to please God." Notice the word *impossible*. You cannot please God without faith. It is impossible. Faith is the work of God. In John 6:28, the disciples asked Jesus, "What must we do to do the works God requires?" Jesus answered, "The work of God is this: to believe in the one he has sent" (v. 29). True faith will always produce good works, but they will be works prompted by the Holy Spirit, not our flesh. This belief in Christ, who is God in the flesh, is more than mere mental assent. It's a deep trust in His provision at the Cross and in His goodness in our every situation.

During the course of our lives we will find ourselves, because of our fallen world, in situations and circumstances where we must determine by faith to believe God. We must believe, not because we are getting anything out of it or we're going to live through it, and not because it looks like we can explain it, but because He said He is faithful. We choose to declare, "God is faithful," even if we are sawn in two. It was Job who said, "Though He slay me, yet will I trust Him" (Job 13:15 NKJV).

Remember those three Hebrew men, Shadrach, Meshach, and Abednego? They declared in faith before being thrown into the furnace, "The God we serve is able to save us.... But even if he does not, we want you to know, O king, that we will not serve your gods or worship the image of gold you have set up" (Dan. 3:17–18). These guys made a choice to declare God's goodness despite their circumstances.

What a Wonder

Liz Walker, a Southern lady if ever there was one, is also one of the most respected and well-known Bible teachers in our area. She is a frequent speaker for churches and retreats across the country. One day, her elderly father and mother were involved in a car accident that left her mother needing constant care. Overnight, the whole family was thrust into the role of caregiver. Suddenly, Liz's teaching ministry was curtailed, as most of her time was consumed by caring for her mother. That was over five years ago and she is still caring for her. But like Johnny Nicosia, Liz's faith is stronger than ever and her words are life-changing.

Her mother can do nothing but lie in her bed. She can't speak. She can move only one hand and one leg a little. She has to be turned every two hours, fed by a feeding tube, and has a tracheostomy to breathe. She's existing, alive with her full faculties, trapped in a body that doesn't work. Her activities consist of moving from the bed to the chair, bed to the chair, bed to the chair, twenty-four hours a day.

Yet in the midst of this, Liz encourages her mother by saying, "Mother, you are here on this bed doing the greatest work you've ever done for the kingdom of God. What you're doing now is more important than all the Bible studies you've taught and all the praying and witnessing you did. This is your greatest work."

What does Liz mean by that? Sometimes our greatest work for God is done in the most implausible of situations. You see, most of us want to serve God in great and glorious ways. We want to be used mightily for God, but sometimes what we consider a great work is quite different than what God thinks.

Liz said, "By my mother's acquiescence to God's goodness in her situation, she is exalting and choosing to declare

His glory before all of His enemies—before all of His servants and all of His creation as she has never done before. She believes God is alive, that He is doing what He wants done.

"Because of her steadfast trust, angels are bending low with furrowed brows, wondering what on earth God is doing with that little bit of human flesh lying in that bed. But when they see her declaration of God's truth and faithfulness, they gaze in wonder and awe. All of God's enemies watch her and grit their teeth in frustration that they are not able to get her to doubt God or curse God and die as Job's wife suggested. Whatever it is—worlds, kingdoms, creations, systems—they look in awe and say, 'Oh, what a great God she must serve if He was able to subdue her with the force of His love. What a wonder He must be.'"

It's in these tough situations we are given a chance to believe God is who He says He is. Not because we are experiencing it, but because we choose to. Hebrews 12:1 says, "We are surrounded by such a great cloud of witnesses." Never do we serve God more than when we accept what He's permitted to come into our lives without resentment.

Liz told me she remembers one night when her mother was in the nursing home—the horror, the smell, the urgency, the weariness, and the sheer awfulness of her mother lying there. She remembers telling the Lord that she felt so helpless, disappointed, and horror-stricken, but didn't want to just grit her teeth and endure till it was over. "I wanted to gather up everything that was good in the middle of it," she said. "Yes, I wanted it over as quickly as possible, but I didn't want to miss the good God was doing by being bowled over with what I hated, by what was bad. I knew there were good things in this circumstance, but I didn't see them at first. So I cried out for God to show me, that I couldn't see them because I was hurting too badly.

"And God started showing me things. I'd be going around Mama's bed at night. She'd be in dire pain and I didn't know if she was going to die. It was late at night and there was nobody to call on. I was crying to God, 'Lord, I praise You for this.' I'd say, 'Mama, God's good. He's giving us grace and strength. Our Lord is right here with us.' In the middle of crisis you extol the character of God—you don't beg to get out."

In our interview Liz said that she believes everything goes back to the Garden of Eden. It all happened there when Satan accused God to the first humans—*God's not good. He's a liar, and He doesn't do what He says* (Genesis 3). In the book of Job, it's reversed. Satan accused a human to God. *God, You know Your servant Job is not as good as You think he is. If You take away his blessings he will surely curse You* (Job 1:9–11). Job didn't know everything that was going on. He didn't know the background. Job was given the opportunity to despair of God's good character and wisdom; yet he would not sin with his mouth. He would not join Satan in his accusations against God. Yes, he pondered. He puzzled. He whined and brought questions. He wanted to reason with God, but he never did curse Him.

Interestingly, Liz's conclusion was almost exactly that of Johnny Nicosia. She said, "God loved my mother and me enough that He has entrusted His character and His reputation to us by allowing us to be in this situation that we may demonstrate that we choose God and declare He is good."

When You Just Want Out

What about you? Have you found yourself in a situation where you must choose to trust God? In your heart of hearts, you desperately want to let go and trust—to "cast(ing)... your care upon Him" (1 Peter 5:7 NKJV), but you are afraid. Your circumstances scream to the contrary. Someone told me once, "Yeah, I can trust God—to push me off a cliff!" Is that you, my friend? If it is, don't buy the lie. God is a God who cares and is deeply concerned, but we have to choose. If you can't make that choice yet, that's okay, but read on.

Liz's words are profound and sound. King David mirrored her thoughts in Psalm 55:4–7 (NKJV): "My heart is severely pained within me, and the terrors of death have fallen upon me. Fearfulness and trembling have come upon me, and horror has overwhelmed me. So I said, 'Oh, that I had wings like a dove! I would fly away and be at rest. Indeed, I would wander far off, and remain in the wilderness.'"

David's pain was so great that he just wanted out. How many of us feel that way? How many have tried to get out by substance abuse or other methods of dulling pain? For some it's a plethora of activity. Others just check out emotionally or actually relocate, thinking getting away will solve their problems.

David had all those thoughts. He knew what it was to be on top, but he also knew suffering—what it was to be at rock bottom. And though David lamented much about his pain, he always returned to his trust in God. At rock bottom, he chose to throw himself in desperate dependence upon the mercy of God—to declare God's faithfulness when circumstances screamed to the contrary. In Psalm 55:22 (NKJV), David, when all seemed lost and nothing made sense, concluded, "Cast your burden on the LORD, and He shall sustain you; He shall never permit the righteous to be moved."

Liz Walker, her mother lying in that bed, John the Baptist, King David, and the guy sawn in two all chose, by faith, to extol the character of God. When we follow their example we too will experience God's best in life's toughest situations.

"Though He slay me, yet will I trust Him."
—*Job (Job 13:15 NKJV)*

CHAPTER FOUR

PRACTICAL INSIGHTS FROM JOB

"Consider the most common curse word in the English language: 'God' followed by the word 'damn.' People say it not only in the face of great tragedy, but also when their cars won't start.... The oath renders an instinctive judgment that life ought to be fair and that God should somehow 'do a better job' of running his world."
—*Philip Yancey*

By all standards, Job was considered a wealthy man. His personal holdings consisted of seven thousand sheep, three thousand camels, five hundred yoke of oxen, five hundred donkeys, a vast number of servants, and a large, healthy family. His land probably had to consist of a bare minimum of ten thousand acres and a huge estate or compound to house his servants. In those days, oxen, camels, and donkeys were as much in demand as automobiles are today, so it's likely that Job had amassed his fortune from raising and selling these animals. Seven thousand sheep could supply a whole region with wool for clothing.

Businesswise, we could compare Job to a Bill Gates or a Sam Walton. He was as big as they get. According to Scripture, Job was "the greatest man among all the people of the East" (Job 1:3). Yet unlike many other wealthy people, he remained humble in heart, realizing that his success was a direct result of God's gracious provision. Job was a righteous man. He obeyed God, was a loving, committed husband and father, and was ethical in his business dealings. Job was doing "all the right things."

Then one day (don't you hate those days?) Job's life abruptly took a series of ill-fated turns. In rapid succession, bam, bam, bam—tragedy struck. First, bandits attacked and killed his servants working in the fields and stole a large number of animals. Then an out-of-control wildfire burned the sheep and fields in which they were grazing. Another group of bandits formed three parties and stole all his camels, killing their caretakers in the process. And finally, a fierce desert storm blew down the home of his eldest son, killing all his children, who were gathered there. Only his wife was left. In the midst of his grief, Job became weak and his skin broke out in boils.

After the dust settled, Job found himself penniless, sick, and grief-stricken. He had now experienced it all, from wealth, health, and happiness to financial ruin, sickness, and grief. Job had hit rock bottom. All of this adversity, I must add, was completely out of his control.

Job's pain was so great that he cried out, "If only my anguish could be weighed and all my misery be placed on the scales! It would surely outweigh the sand of the seas.... I have no peace, no quietness; I have no rest, but only turmoil.... My eyes will never see happiness again.... Why did I not perish at birth?" (Job 6:2–3; 3:26; 7:7; 3:11). To say that Job was hurting is an understatement. The man was in pain.

And even though our trials probably haven't reached the level of Job's, how many of us have experienced similar thoughts? You don't want to do anything. You sense you are wasting away. Your deepest wish is to be restored to normality and to find release. You want to move forward with life, yet somehow you're trapped in a deep, dark, jagged pit of despondency. You've tried climbing out on your own, but your limbs, which represent your burdens, are so heavy. Sometimes you just want to let go and fall deeper into the pit. Giving up often seems easier than facing another day. And the future—*what* future? Your life is in limbo. You can't visualize hopes or dreams—just pain. That was Job's lot. He was in agony, physically and mentally.

Friends

Then, right smack-dab in the middle of all his suffering, when he thought things couldn't possibly get worse, they did. Three friends showed up at his doorstep to comfort him and offer their words of advice. Oh, boy. When Job's comforters tried to help, instead of easing, his pain intensified! Job responded to his comforters by saying, "How long will you ... crush me with words?

… Will your long-winded speeches never end?… Will you never get enough of my flesh?" (Job 19:2; 16:3; 19:22).

I don't know about you, but man, can I relate! When we're going through adversity, there are always people who think they have the answers to our troubles. They're convinced it's their mission to comfort us with their often self-righteous, judgmental, and misguided wisdom. Sometimes they're direct, but more than likely they slip in a cutting remark here or a damaging comment there, oblivious to, or not caring about, the emotional damage they are causing.

Most of the time these comforters have no clue what is really going on in our personal lives, but they really think they are helping. Usually these people are sincere. Before bashing Job, one of his friends said, "But now, Job, listen to my words.… My words come from an upright heart; my lips sincerely speak what I know" (Job 33:1–3). Then he began to tell Job what he had done wrong to have been so beset by misfortune and what he needed to do to recover.

Yes, Job's comforters were sincere. But guess what? They were sincerely wrong! How do I know? At the end of the Book of Job, God didn't rebuke Job for his pain or even his honest questions of God. Instead, He rebuked Eliphaz, the leader of the so-called comforters, by saying, "I am angry with you and with your two friends, because you have not spoken of me what is right" (Job 42:7). Even though the comforters were convinced they were speaking for God, they were not.

Job's comforters, at first, truly empathized with him. They were so overwhelmed by his condition that "no one said a word to him, because they saw how great his suffering was"

(Job 2:13). Then they cried alongside him for seven days. That's the best thing they did, and it was the right thing. People who are hurting don't need our lectures or sermons. They need our grace, hope, compassion, practical help, and support. Just being there and available to them is probably the greatest thing we can do: Become a support to lean on. Encourage those in pain to take one small step at a time, with small, positive pictures of reality. Help them realize the success to be achieved in day-to-day tasks.

Time to Move On?

Job's friends empathized with him for a week. As time passed, however, and Job did not come around as quickly as they thought he should, their support turned to criticism. I can picture the scene vividly in my mind: One of Job's comforters may have said something like, "Okay, Job, you've grieved, you've cried, now it's time to move on. It's time to snap out of it and pull yourself up by your bootstraps." When Job didn't respond to his friends' urgings, they began to try to "fix" him. The problem with Job at this stage, and with most people who are experiencing deep pain, is that he *couldn't* pull themselves up by their bootstraps. Job himself admitted this when he asked his friends, "Do I have any power to help myself?" (Job 6:13). The implication was "No, I don't."

Healing takes time, and that's okay. Each person has his or her own timetable for restoration. This time isn't a license to give up and wallow in self-pity, but rather a time for cleansing. It is important to give sufficient time to the grieving process and let pain perform its function. If we don't grieve properly over a loss, we may carry guilt or bitterness or anger inside of us the rest of our lives.

Also, Job's friends assumed that because they were not suffering as Job was, they were somehow more upright and moral than he was. Isn't it interesting that when we are physically and mentally well and are experiencing success we sometimes believe we are just a little better than those who aren't? As though we must be doing something right—we made all the right choices, and it's paying off. It's very subtle, but I assure you, we do it. When you find yourself thinking those thoughts, beware. You or someone you love may need help and compassion one day.

The truth is that Job had done nothing wrong, nor had he made any bad decisions. In contrast to the angry rebuke God gave Job's comforters, read what is written of Job himself: "Job...was blameless and upright.... In all this [adversity], Job did not sin by charging God with wrongdoing" (Job 1:1, 22). Yet his friends were certain Job had screwed up. Then, to make a point, God told Job's friends to admit their "folly" (42:8). God calls their know-it-all counsel folly! Then He tells them to get Job to pray for them. Talk about a slap in the face for Job's comforters—after all their pious words. After that, God told them that He would accept Job's prayer, because he had done what was right (42:8).

Just because we are experiencing painful situations in our lives doesn't necessarily mean we are doing something wrong or have a lack of faith. Our natural tendency, though, is to take on false guilt that is often magnified by others. Remember that there is a delicate balance between taking personal responsibility and taking on false guilt.

Storms Happen

A dear friend of mine battled lung cancer for over two years. Eventually, the cancer got the best of him, and he died at the young age of fifty-five. During his bout with this ruthless opponent, he read Scripture, prayed, stood by faith, and praised God. He was a man of deep faith. Yet as the disease began to take a greater toll, he began to feel guilty. One night, in desperation, almost in a panic attack, he called me and sought assurance that God hadn't abandoned him. He felt he must be doing something wrong or he would be winning the fight. I tried to reassure him that God did love him and that the Scriptures plainly show that the storms of life come to both the just and the unjust. Storms happen.

Not only had Job not done anything wrong, he also understood that the issue was between himself and God and that his friends had no right to judge him. After one critical comment, Job told one friend, "I have a mind as well as you; I am not inferior to you.… If it is true that I have gone astray, my error remains my concern alone" (Job 12:3; 19:4). In other words, "I can think for myself. Stop trying to think for me. And please don't comfort me!"

Job accepted responsibility for his situation. He was willing to, and he did examine himself. But Job also knew the difference between personal responsibility and self-mutilation. He knew his position before God and fell on God's mercy in desperate dependence. Job had enough confidence and security to know his own heart. False guilt is an enemy that wants to push us over the edge so that we are immobilized by our mistakes, misfortunes, and pain.

Though their comments were surely painful, Job let his friends' pieties roll off of him like water rolling off a duck's back. Then, after he settled the issues with his so-called comforters, he directed his attention to a heart-to-heart dialogue with God. This is important. *Job knew whom not to listen to, but he also knew absolutely whom to listen to—God.* He also knew that God was listening to him—that He was available in the midst of the storm. In his heart-to-heart with the Almighty, Job unloaded all his questions, doubts, fears, anger, and frustrations on God. Job was not afraid to be honest with God.

How about you? What's your trauma? Have you lost your job or a loved one? Are you handicapped? Divorced? Disappointed? Betrayed? Do you feel as if you have been ripped off by life? Do you secretly entertain questions directed at God that you are afraid to ask out loud for fear of seeming faithless, unspiritual, cynical, or even blasphemous? Are you bitter at someone or some circumstance in your life? Do you feel as Job did—as if you are all alone, yet surrounded by many inspecting eyes?

Most of us have been taught through the years never to question God. To do so means a serious lack of faith. After all, we have been told, "God works all things together for good to those that love Him." Or "God is using all our hardships for the purpose of refining us." Now don't misunderstand me. I fervently believe these statements are true. There is hope in God. God is our only hope.

Miserable Comforters Are You All

Sometimes, though, it is difficult to discern the "good" that happens when people die of cancer, have been killed in accidents, or are seriously handicapped. To the person who is tragically hurting, Scriptures and slogans initially appear superficial or removed from the real issues of the heart. The story of Job affirms this. His so-called comforters' theological and psychological arguments actually defended God. They sounded absolutely correct. They made good points, each with an element of truth in it. Let me paraphrase some of the half-truths they pointed out to Job as he agonized.

"Shhh, Job. Don't say such things! God doesn't like that. Only speak positive faith statements." Positive confession is fine. I personally believe it can transform a life. But stuffing our true feelings can produce false guilt, leading us to think that God is displeased if we don't always say the "right things" rather than being open and honest with Him. Besides, God knows our feelings anyway, doesn't He? He's God. Honesty before God is for our benefit, not His.

"Search your heart, Job. You must have some hidden sin. God rewards us for righteousness and punishes us when we deserve it. Job, if you will confess your sin and correct your ways, God will restore you." Although our sin certainly does produce consequences and God hates it, false guilt comes upon us when we believe God is punishing us every time something bad happens. Remember, Jesus plainly said, "In the world you will have tribulation."

"God is trying to teach you something, Job. Learn from this. You should feel honored, not angry. Remember to praise God in the midst of this." Though each trauma we go through is ultimately an opportunity for growth and God is using it to develop our Christlikeness, comments like these lead us to believe that if we don't respond in a certain way, if praises

don't automatically flow out, we are displeasing God or lack faith. They also imply that God delights in putting us through painful trials just to teach us something. Nothing could be further from the truth. We experience most of our trials simply because we live in a mixed-up, crazy, fallen world.

Of course, God uses these things to teach us, but God also hurts when we hurt. I love the words of the late Roy Hicks Jr.: "God has not given up on you even though you have yet to lift your voice in praise about the painful drubbing that has happened to you. God has not abandoned you. He's not docking you for not being someone else."[5]

"God helps those who help themselves, Job." This comment also seems rational and good. The problem is that often we can't help ourselves. We might need more time and sometimes even professional help. But what we absolutely can't handle in those times of pain is critical judgment.

All these points offered by Job's comforters sounded right and good in themselves, yet even God rebuked them. God corrected these people for saying good things about Him. I want you to get this point: Just because an argument may be sound, or even correct, doesn't mean it's the right thing to say to a person in pain. Job's response to the points made by his comforters was, "I have heard many things like these; miserable comforters are you all!" (Job 16:2). Job had already heard it. He knew all the religious jargon. It wasn't anything new. It just wasn't helping him any.

Concerning Job's comforters, Philip Yancey, in his book *Disappointment with God,* wrote, "The book of Job plainly shows that such 'helpful advice' does nothing to answer questions of the person in pain. It was the wrong medicine, dispensed at the wrong time."[6]

Frequently, the pressing issue if you are in pain is not whether God is making you stronger or working this out for your good, but rather how to deal with these lingering questions about God that challenge the very core of everything you believe. "How can I ever trust God again?" "God, where are You?" "Why even pray?" "God, if You are so good, how could You allow this to happen?" The questions are endless. And the pain? It immobilizes us. We just want relief. Even Jesus, when hanging on the cross, cried out in His humanity, "My God, my God, why have you forsaken me?"(Matt. 27:46).

One of the overwhelming messages of the story of Job is that it's okay to dump on God all your questions, doubts, anger, guilt, grief, or whatever. God can handle it. God wants you to be honest with Him. The thing God doesn't want us to do is block Him out—to ignore Him and turn within ourselves. God desires a relationship with us. And a healthy relationship has honest communication.

Honestly!

Job was in intense pain. He had honest questions and com plaints, but he took them to God. Job asked God, "Does it please you to oppress me, to spurn the work of your hands, while you smile on the schemes of the wicked?" (Job 10:3). Can you hear the sense of injustice Job felt toward God? Job was dreadfully honest in his pain. Yet in that honesty, he also knew and trusted that God was still his only hope. He said, "I know that my Redeemer lives....Yet will I hope in him.... Indeed, this will turn out for my deliverance" (Job 19:25; 13:15–16).

Finally, after Job's comforters had raised all the arguments and Job had aired his complaints and confidences to God, God arrived on the scene in a whirlwind. God began to question Job: "Where were you when I laid the earth's foundation?... Does the hawk take flight by your wisdom and spread his wings toward the south? Does the eagle soar at your command?..." (Job 38:4; 39:26–27). In other words, "I am God, Job, and you are not." Job finally responded to God, "Surely I spoke of things I did not understand, things too wonderful for me to know.... I ... repent in dust and ashes" (Job 42:3, 6). Job very much needed to air his frustrations to God. It was healthy. Yet he ultimately recognized that God was not obligated to give him all the answers to his questions. Likewise, we will not always have clear black-and-white answers to our questions. And that is okay. As humans, we now understand only in part. We see through a glass dimly. But one day we shall understand fully.

Despite Job's honesty with God during his suffering, in the end God commended him while his comforters were rebuked. Why? Because even in his anger and frustration, even when he questioned God, Job communicated honestly with Him. The comforters, on the other hand, uttered many correct and impressive statements. Job talked directly to God; they only talked about God.

> "I know that my Redeemer lives....
> Yet will I hope in him.... Indeed, this
> will turn out for my deliverance."
> —Job (Job 19:25; 13:15–16)

CHAPTER FIVE

CONDUITS OF COMFORT

> "There is nothing worse than a life filled with
> adversity from which nothing good ever comes."
> —*Charles Stanley*

For those living in desperate dependence, every problem or tragedy, regardless of its scope, holds within itself a seed that promises new and deeper life. We must heed Robert Schuller's advice by letting God turn our scars into stars and our hurts into halos. And while Schuller's advice may seem somewhat cliché, it is exactly the business God is in. Consider the words from 2 Corinthians 1:3–4 (emphasis added): "Praise be to the God and Father of our Lord Jesus Christ, the Father of compassion and the God of all comfort, *who comforts us in all our troubles, so that we can comfort those in any trouble with the comfort we ourselves have received from God."*

The great need in the world today is not for more gifted people or more talented people, but for more broken people, for God delights in taking cracked vessels, comforting them, and then using those vessels to bring comfort to a dying world. We become conduits by which His healing virtue flows.

Simply traveling through painful circumstances, however, does not qualify us to be conduits of His comfort. We must lay ourselves open, admit our weakness, then allow God to pour His grace into us. Receiving God's grace, and releasing anger, bitterness, and resentment is our choice. If we hang on to it, it becomes poison to us. The one work we are called to do is simply receive. We can choose to be conduits of healing or we can choose to be conduits of bitterness. One of the highest triumphs in life is when, in the midst of life's most challenging trials, we allow ourselves to become conduits that pump life into others rather than being victims that drain life from others. Only God can do this in us. Trying to be a conduit in our own strength will only leave us frustrated, bitter, and empty.

If we desperately depend upon God as our source of comfort, He promises to take the darkest and most hopeless situations in our lives and turn them into places of ministry and refreshment. Psalm 84:5–6 declares, "Blessed are those whose strength is in you, who have set their hearts on pilgrimage. As they [God's people] pass through the Valley of

Baca [Valley of Weeping], they make it a place of springs."
What a powerful passage! These people know the Lord as
the deliverer and sustainer of their lives. Their heart is set on
pilgrimage—of going wherever the Lord takes them via
whatever route He chooses. Sometimes it's around the pain,
and other times it's through the pain. If we're armed with
this attitude, God promises that He will turn the very valley
of weeping—of pain and disappointment—into a place of
springs. What do springs do? They provide life and refreshment to parched people.

Springs in the Desert

Envision with me for a moment: You've been stranded in the
driest, most barren desert without food or water. You're
searching and fumbling for a way out—but nothing. Every
direction in which you wander leads only to more wasteland.
The sun has been beating down upon your skin and you are
dehydrated. Weakness is upon you and you can feel the
shadow of death stalking.

"God, where are You?" you cry. You feel alone—abandoned—almost betrayed—as if your cries are falling from
your lips and being sucked into the dirt below your feet.
"God…help…please!"

Then, up ahead—there. You think you see water. Yes,
you're sure it's water. "Thank You, God! Thank You for Your
provision!" Falling down, you scoop up a handful of water,
but when your hands meet your mouth you realize it was only
an illusion. It's not water, but more scorched dirt. Your teeth
grind against the grains of sand and you frantically spit them

out—now thirstier than before. "God, what kind of a cruel joke was that?" you mumble.

Disappointed and angry you wearily pick up one foot and place it in front of the other and move on, not knowing how much farther you can go. If you could, you would just lie there and let death come. It would be a relief. But you have to move on. People are depending on you. There are bills to be paid and mouths to feed. "God, how could You let this happen? I thought You loved me! Why have You deserted me? Perhaps You're not even there."

Before you finish your deliberation you think you see something—bubbles coming up from the dirt. "Could it be water this time?" You shake your head. "No. It's not water. It can't be. It's just my imagination—just wishful thinking. God had His chance before and let me down." You actually turn and trudge in the opposite direction, away from the spring. "I'm not going to risk trusting again—risk being disappointed." Reluctantly, you glance back. "But I sure am thirsty. Not to mention that I'm dying! I'm desperate! Maybe, just maybe, I can trust God again."

With one last push of faith you spin around and stumble awkwardly toward the bubbles in the sand. At your feet you can't believe your eyes. It's water! Only a trickle, but nonetheless—clean, clear, cold, water! Again you fall on your knees, this time slightly afraid because of your last disappointment, yet you dig recklessly in the dirt around the trickle like a dog digging for a bone. And then it happens. The spring bubbles up and out of the ground, flourishing. You thrust your face into the flow and lap up, again and again, the real, cool, refreshing water. You have your strength back. You're refreshed and can move on in the wilderness until you need God to provide another spring.

Springs in the desert are like that. They're places of refreshment and nourishment in hot, parched places. When we let God refill and refresh us, we are not just renewed, but we become springs of life and refreshment to others as well. Have you ever met someone like that? Someone who, when you are in his or her presence, makes you feel as if you are taking a drink from a refreshing spring?

The Valley of the Shadow

If you sat down with my friend Sidney you would find her engaging, attractive, professional, and overflowing with God's presence in an inviting, but not overpowering, way. She is one of those refreshing people. Sidney has been a follower of Christ for over twenty-five years and is a consultant for a large medical center. Just looking at her, you would never imagine that at one time she prayed to die and seriously considered taking her own life. But now she is most definitely a conduit, bringing God's love and healing power to those who come in contact with her.

As young people, Sidney and her husband were serving Christ faithfully as missionaries in Mexico. It was there, on the mission field, that she discovered he was having an affair. After the divorce, she married for a second time to another committed Christian. Soon she discovered that he too had been cheating on her. After grieving, growing, and learning from her mistakes, she carefully and prayerfully remarried a third time to a gentleman who was a pillar in the church and had a loving family who adopted her. But after just twenty months, he told her he didn't want to be married any longer.

Sidney was shocked, and in counseling with her pastor, discovered that her third husband had also been unfaithful to her with several women. Sidney told me she thought divorce was not supposed to happen to people who serve God. And after three divorces, she felt like not just a second-class citizen, but a no-class citizen.

"In the church," she said, "I would have been forgiven quicker if I would have murdered my husband and asked for forgiveness than going through a divorce, let alone three. I started to see that the Christian army is the only army in the world that shoots its own wounded. Everyone else brings their wounded off the battlefield, rushes them into surgery, gets them into physical therapy—whatever they need to heal and get back in the battle. Not the church."

Sidney walked around feeling as if she were a tremendous failure—that she hadn't prayed enough, studied enough, or done something enough. She didn't have a testimony of success. She was desperately broken. And on top of all the guilt she was feeling over her failed marriages, people were telling her that her children were going to fail too. That they were going to get into drugs, that bad things were going to happen to them because she was a single mother. Sidney was living in anxiety and fear. But instead of giving up, she cried out, "God, I'm desperate for Your comfort."

Because of her experiences, Sidney believed something must be terribly, terribly wrong with her—that she must be flawed because why else would three husbands see other women while married to her? "I admit I made some stupid decisions based on hurt and anger," Sidney said. "During that time, I thought I would never survive the grief, shame, and pain. So, I would go to bed at night asking God to 'please take me before I wake up because I won't live through this pain.' I started losing weight. I lost forty pounds in a matter of weeks. I couldn't eat. I was having anxiety attacks. I thought I was having a heart attack."

Sidney's pain was so intense she was sure she didn't want to live anymore, and she thought about ways to end her life. She felt her life was over, that God would never be able to use her again. But she had children and grandchildren and she didn't want them to have to live with the burden of her suicide. So instead of killing herself, she went through the motions of life like an unfeeling robot.

Yet God was faithful and never gave up on her. He sent Sidney a Christian doctor, a Christian attorney, and a Christian counselor, and all three told her the same things not knowing what the other was telling her. And during this time a woman called Sidney's house several times. The woman didn't know Sidney very well and knew nothing of her past. However, she told Sidney that the Lord had put her on her heart to pray for, that she was "dying of a broken heart." When the woman told Sidney that, she began to open up.

That same week, Sidney's stepmother called and asked her what was wrong, that she had been awakened in the middle of the night to pray for her. God used people like that to keep Sidney from killing herself.

Now, years later, God is using Sidney to reach out to other hurting people. For example, when she went to work for the cancer center, a woman came into her office. She had a stunned look on her face because she had just been diagnosed with cancer. And she said to Sidney, "I don't understand. I've been a good person all my life. I've been in the church for all of these years. I've paid tithe. I've given." The woman started listing all the things she'd done. "And I don't understand why I have cancer," she finally added. Sidney turned around and looked at her and replied, "You know, just because you have cancer doesn't mean that He is not God and that He doesn't care. I know what it is to walk through the valley of the shadow of death. I know what it is to experience the dark night of the soul. I know what it is to go to bed at night praying that God would just take me. You don't want to wake up because the pain of what you are experiencing is too great to comprehend. I know what it is to wake up in the night with anxiety and terror gripping your heart because of fear of the unknown."

The woman looked at Sidney and said, "Oh, my gosh. You've just explained everything I've gone through. You've had cancer."

"No ma'am," Sidney answered. "I haven't had cancer, but I know what it is to be devastated to where you don't know how you can go on living. And I know what it is to experience the keeping grace of God and the love of God that never abandons you, because He says He will never leave us nor forsake us. And that means He will not abandon us."

When the three Hebrew young men went into the fire, the only things that burned were the cords that bound them. They walked out of that furnace without the fetters that restricted them when they went in. God let Sidney see that in her past she was compromising her real self in order to make those men love her, but God loved her just the way she was, with all her flaws and weaknesses. And He showed her that she wasn't just surviving while she was going through that ordeal. No, God was shaping her character to more closely resemble His own.

"When we go through incredibly difficult situations, we think we are just surviving," she said, "until we get through it and look back and God shows us all the ways He has kept us and taught us."

Since then, God has used Sidney in extraordinary ways to bring comfort and counsel to many. And God finally brought the right man into her life. She's been happily married for many years to another wounded but triumphant warrior.

Progress in Prison

The inspiring story of John Bunyan is another powerful example of how God can use us as conduits, despite our painful ordeals. In 1660, Bunyan was a well-known preacher in Bedford, England. Because his teachings ran contrary to the political laws of the Church of England, he was arrested and thrown into prison. Common sense said his ministry was over. But Bunyan turned his suffering over to God and let the prison cell become a spring of refreshment.

While restricted to his cell from 1660 to 1672 (twelve

years!), instead of decaying there, he became a conduit and wrote *The Pilgrim's Progress*. Save the Bible, probably no other Christian book has been more widely read or has encouraged more people in their faith. By allowing God to use him despite his difficult circumstances, Bunyan wrote a Christian classic that millions would read for centuries to come.[7]

Over the Humps

God will do amazing things with our pain if we let Him. Not only will He use us for helping people through their dark nights of the soul or to write classic literature, but when we choose to let God use us as conduits of His comfort, sometimes our sufferings direct us toward a practical vocational calling as well.

A man I work out with at a local health club has a daughter with scoliosis. One day, he and I were discussing the pain we feel as parents of children with disabilities. Actually, I was the one unloading on him. I was having an unusually difficult time dealing with the fact that my son cannot hear. I firmly believe that God plants people in our daily paths for our encouragement—to help us get over the humps. This gentleman did so for me that day.

With a smile on his face—not a shallow smile, but a smile from experience, a confident smile—he said, "You're probably having a much harder time with James' deafness than he is."

I nodded that he was probably right.

"You know," he continued, "the pain of watching my daughter suffer, all twisted in those leg braces almost did me in. Several times over the years, I almost lost it emotionally."

Then he smiled again. "But God knows what He is doing. Would you believe that today she is a nurse at the children's hospital in Houston? Guess what she does?"

"Works with children with scoliosis?" I questioned in response.

"Bingo. And she loves it. It's her calling in life."

Remember, in every trial or circumstance that we face, we have the choice to either stagnate and die or let God channel our pain and fly. When we cling to Christ in desperate dependence and let Him use our pain, we cease being victims of life and become conduits for giving life. This is the highest form of achievement.

> "Blessed are those that mourn,
> for they shall be comforted."
> —*Jesus (Matt. 5:4 NKJV)*

CHAPTER SIX

LIVING ON PURPOSE

"For life is life only when it is
the carrying out of God's purpose."
—*Leo Tolstoy*

I agree with Tolstoy. There is nothing more important in life than living on purpose. That is, living out what we were divinely created for. I've always thought it would be extremely tragic to come to the end of my life only to look back and realize that I had missed my purpose for being—that I didn't accomplish what God had set out for me to do. But so many people wonder, "What is God's will for my life?" I cannot tell you how many times over the years I've been asked that question or been told the following:

"I wish God would show me His will for my life."

"I've been seeking God's will for years and I get nothing."

"Why doesn't God speak to me as He speaks to other people and let me know what He wants me to do?"

"It seems that my life is so mundane, that I don't have any significance."

Called to Write

Personally, when I was seventeen years old, I felt God leading me to become an author. It's hard to explain, but I knew deep down in my spirit that writing was what I was supposed to do. I feel, along with Marjorie Holmes, that "writing is less a profession than a compulsion—a calling."[8] For over twenty-five years God has not let me quit the pursuit and periodically gives me supernatural confirmations that keep me in the game, even though the odds are sometimes stacked against me. I share one of these stories in chapter 11.

Why did God call me to write? I have no idea. In high school I struggled pitifully in English, getting Ds. I hated reading and began college on academic probation. If you would have asked someone who knew me back then, "Who is the last person on earth you would ever think would one day be a writer?" quite possibly he or she would have said, "Max Davis." Maybe that's why God called me. Who knows? Doesn't Scripture say, "God has chosen the foolish things of the world to put to shame the wise, and God has chosen the weak things of the world to put to shame the things which are mighty" (1 Cor. 1:27 NKJV)?

Of course, I'm being a bit facetious. I do love writing...

now. Today I get great fulfillment from reading, researching, and writing. And it's not just the gratification from seeing my books in print, but I actually thrive on the whole writing process. Back when I started, I pursued writing because I felt God's leading, not because I understood what He was doing.

When my daughter started her freshman year of college we had her take one of those personality/career profiles to give us insight into her abilities and interests. My wife had taken the test when she was in college and it helped her significantly. So, just for fun, my wife did a profile on me. Guess what the profile said I was suited for? Yep. You guessed it. Writing. God knew me better than I knew myself. He called me before I knew all of the ins and outs of the career. He called me when I hated going to the library and thought of writers as nerds. God could see what I would become and am still becoming. But I am also acutely aware that if God's grace is not on me during a writing project, it's not going to happen.

Yes, God does call us to specific tasks and gives us special grace to carry them out. He called Solomon to build a temple, Nehemiah to build a wall, Moses to lead a people, Joseph to save a civilization, and Noah to build a boat. But what about people who have no real conviction about their life's purpose—who feel they have no special gifts or callings? They're not going to the jungles of Bolivia or singing, like angels before crowds. They're just ordinary, run-of-the-mill folk. Or what if they do have gifts, but instead of having an outlet for them, they have become trapped in seemingly insignificant or mundane jobs? Or maybe, like some, they've found themselves shut in with an illness or in the role of caregiver for a sick child or parent like Liz Walker in chapter 3? So much of our lives appears to be by dictated by chance rather than choice.

A People That Look Like Jesus

Although accomplishing a task is important and we must not take lightly God's call for us to achieve, these tasks are not our central purpose for being. For years I didn't understand this and was driven by an unquenchable need to "do" for God. It was a freeing day when I realized that my number-one purpose for being is not to write best-sellers, or nurture a great church, or be successful in business, or even to evangelize the lost, but to simply *become*. God is much more interested in what we are than in what we do. His goal is that we be conformed to the image of Christ. Everything He is doing in us is to uncover our weaknesses—not to make us weak, for we are already weak, but to open our eyes to our true condition and what we were created to be—helplessly dependent upon Him to make us like Himself. That's why the apostle Paul said, "When I am weak, then I am strong" (2 Cor. 12:10).

Romans 8:28 confirms that we have "been called according to his purpose," and His purpose for us is "to be conformed to the likeness of his Son." Understanding this is vital because it brings clarity to our suffering and answers the question "why?" Not the question "Why is my son deaf?" or "Why did my daughter die?" or "Why did I develop cancer?" or "When will I ever be free of this mundane rut I'm in?" But it does answer, "Why was I created?" and "Why am I here, and what is my purpose?" The circumstances of life often limit us from *doing*, but they never limit us from *becoming,* and becoming is what God desires most, because in the end, He wants a people that look like Jesus.

With this mind-set we can see that the person in the bed at the nursing home or checking groceries at Winn-Dixie has just as much purpose as the missionary in the jungles of New Guinea—different roles, but the same ultimate purpose. Our primary purpose is to be in an intimate relationship with God and to become like Jesus in our attitudes and character. Everything else—positions, gifts, careers, callings, and vocations—is simply a matter of God's grace. God created me because He chose to share Himself and the perfection of His love. He has called me to enjoy Himself.

We live in a society that is enamored with doing and being "somebody." So when we are cut off from our great plans because of life's trials, it's a big blow to our egos. This is true because we define ourselves largely by what others say and think about us. We are all tied up in what we do—we are human doers instead of human beings. All of a sudden when we are not "doing" anymore, we see ourselves as nobodies.

We see this all the time when people retire. Many people identify so strongly with what they did that when they can't do it anymore, they simply die. It's because they didn't understand their ultimate purpose. When our activities are suddenly curtailed, our purpose in life is defined only by our relationship with the Lord.

Yet it is here that the Lord does His deepest work in us, if we allow Him. Doing great exploits for God is good, assuming God directed us, but such activity produces little

Christlikeness in our character. The purpose for our being here is to have the character of the Father revealed to us and to have our own self revealed to us so that we relax in God and let Him be Himself in us. God's number-one goal is to bring us into the image of Christ. Understanding this puts trials into perspective. It's not about my doing something for God. It's about my becoming the person He desires me to be.

> "Being confident of this, that he who began a
> good work in you will carry it on to completion
> until the day of Christ Jesus."
> —*Paul (Phil. 1:6)*

CHAPTER SEVEN

WHEN PAST
FAILURES HAUNT

"The forgiveness of God is gratuitous
liberation from guilt."
—*Brennan Manning*

In the author's note at the beginning of this book, I point out that in my own struggle for faith I have come to grips with the two little words "all things" in the Scripture that says, "And we know that in *all things* God works for the good of those who love him, who have been called according to his purpose" (Rom. 8:28, emphasis added).

If you've hung around Christian circles for any length of time, you know that we love to quote that passage. It's one of the most popular verses in the Bible. In reality, however, we have a hard time believing that the words "all things" actually mean all things. This is obvious in situations like cancer or the unexpected death of a child. But we also have a hard time with those words when they concern our personal failures, regrets, and sins.

Recipe for Transformation

I remember vividly the day I took my then-sixteen-year-old daughter, Kristen, to get her driver's license. While waiting in the lobby we were seated next to a young man who appeared to be in his mid-twenties. He was polite, but had a sadness about him—as if he were carrying a heavy load. His shoulders drooped, matching the weariness in his eyes.

We spoke with him and learned that several years earlier he had been the driver in an automobile accident that killed his best friend. The young man readily admitted that he had been traveling at an unusually high rate of speed when his car swerved off the road and crashed into a tree. As we talked, it became apparent that the regrets of his past were now dominating his life, offering him no hope for anything good in the future.

Obviously, our sins and mistakes sometimes have terrible consequences. We get hurt. Others get hurt. Sometimes people die. Damage is done. I am in no way minimizing the importance of taking personal responsibility. Yet if you are a Christ follower, if you have sincerely committed your life to Him, you need not live in despair over your past. God is waiting with His grace to wash us, cleanse us, and infuse us with His hope. I like the way Isaiah 1:18 reads in *The Living Bible*. It says, "No matter how deep the stain of your sins, I can take it out and make you as clean as freshly fallen snow. Even if you are stained as red as crimson, I can make you white as wool!"

What's interesting about a stain is that it is more than just a splotch or surface dirt. A stain is ingrained. It's something deep that hangs around long after repeated washings. Sometimes a stain never comes out. In this passage, stains represent our deepest, ugliest, most foolish past. Isaiah is saying it doesn't matter how much or how badly you've failed in your past because God can remove that stain. You may not be able to change the past or eliminate the painful consequences, but God can redirect your future and turn your failures into building blocks for success.

Somehow, in His remarkable way, God cleanses our stains, then takes our failures and regrets and mixes them together in His recipe for our transformation. God never wastes a hurt. Nor does He waste a sin. Oh, He hates sin, but He will even use that for our good. Remember, "all things" means all things.

Perhaps you are like that young man in the lobby. You feel you have messed up so badly that you can never move on. You're stuck in a rut of self-disappointment, unable to get out. Or perhaps you've tried to put the past behind you, but your regrets keep popping up and badgering you, reminding you of how wretched you really are, telling you that you're a hypocrite to even think that you could expect happiness or God's favor. But God doesn't want us to be obsessed with the "what if" syndrome. Once we understand God's sovereignty "what ifs" don't happen. God, in His foreknowledge, is able to turn our mistakes and foolish choices around and work them for His own good purposes and for ours.

Our foolish choices and disruptive pasts are no big surprise to God. Nothing escapes His eye. He doesn't stop us from making choices because He wants us to have free will—the ability to make those choices. It's part of what makes us responding creatures. God doesn't want robots. So, within His sovereignty, He allows us the ability to make stupid choices. He allows them, yet they are not out of His sight. And because He is helping us grow, He lovingly takes those poor choices and reuses them for our good, but only if we let Him. The choice is ours.

The apostle Paul understood this truth more than anyone. Here's a guy who was responsible for the cold-blooded murder of hundreds, maybe thousands, of Christians. Paul was a feared and vengeful man. He was not a nice guy. If anyone had a past, it was Paul, and he openly acknowledged the fact: "Christ Jesus came into the world to save sinners—*of whom I am the worst.* But for that very reason I was shown mercy so that in me, *the worst of sinners,* Christ Jesus might display his unlimited patience as an example" (1 Tim. 1:15–16, emphasis added).

According to Paul, nobody had a past any worse than his. Yet he knew grace. He knew God and was able to say, "But one thing I do: Forgetting what is behind and straining toward what is ahead" (Phil. 3:13). Paul knew that if he wallowed in the pit of despondency over his past failures, it would drag him down, and he would never become what God wanted him to be. The question we should ask is not "How much did I mess up in the past?" but "Where am I headed now? Can I trust God to redeem the rest my life?"

A Victorious Limp

It is important to note that true spiritual cleansing will always be accompanied by a godly sorrow and remorse over our past that leads to meekness, humility, and overwhelming gratefulness to God for His grace. Brennan Manning calls it a *victorious limp*. We live our lives experiencing God's wonderful provision yet ever so aware of what we really deserve. A wonderful portrait of this victorious limp is painted in the story of Mephibosheth.

The Bible gives us few definitions, but it offers many illustrations—portraits if you will, glimpses of God's grace in action. Second Samuel 9 has one of the most vivid illustrations of God's grace in the entire Bible. It's the story of King David and Mephibosheth. To get the full effect, we will have to dissect the whole chapter, but stick with it. It'll be worth it.

> David asked, "Is there anyone still left of the house of Saul to whom I can show kindness for Jonathan's sake?"
>
> Now there was a servant of Saul's household named Ziba. They called him to appear before David, and the king said to him, "Are you Ziba?"
>
> "Your servant," he replied.
>
> The king asked, "Is there no one still left of the house of Saul to whom I can show God's kindness?"
>
> Ziba answered the king, "There is still a son of Jonathan; he is crippled in both feet."
>
> "Where is he?" the king asked.

Ziba answered, "He is at the house of Makir son of Ammiel in Lo Debar."

So King David had him brought from Lo Debar....

When Mephibosheth son of Jonathan, the son of Saul, came to David, he bowed down to pay him honor.

David said, "Mephibosheth!"

"Your servant," he replied.

"Don't be afraid," David said to him, "for I will surely show you kindness for the sake of your father Jonathan. I will restore to you all the land that belonged to your grandfather Saul, and you will always eat at my table."

Mephibosheth bowed down and said, "What is your servant, that you should notice a dead dog like me?"...

And Mephibosheth lived in Jerusalem, because he always ate at the king's table, and he was crippled in both feet. (2 Sam. 9:1–8, 13)

When Mephiboseth was young, his grandfather Saul was king. He had begun his reign by obeying God, but as his reign continued, he became disobedient. Eventually, he became insane. His nerves were so shot that he would have David come and play his harp for him, and then he would throw spears at him.

Jonathan was Saul's son. He was a godly man and didn't like what his father was doing. Jonathan had a son named Mephibosheth, which means "to blow away the shame."

Jonathan was hoping his son would one day clean up the mess that his father had created. So get this picture: Mephibosheth was born to rule and reign. Born to do God's work. Born to blow away the shame. But what happened? Both Saul and Jonathan were killed in battle against the Philistines. After that, David was appointed king.

Traditionally, when one kingdom took over another kingdom, everyone who was part of the previous government was killed to prevent any factions from rising up later against the new king. It's not fair, but it was the way of war. At this point, Saul's people were on the run. They were hiding out and fearing for their lives, Mephibosheth included. He was just a kid—either a baby or a toddler. His nurse was carrying him, and as they were fleeing, she dropped him, possibly off a wall she was climbing over. At any rate, the fall broke Mephibosheth's legs, and they never healed properly, leaving him crippled.

Now here's this guy Mephibosheth. He was born to rule and reign—to blow away the shame. But the fall happened, and instead of fulfilling his destiny, he finds himself crippled and for thirty years living in hiding in a place called Lo Debar in the most remote part of the desert wilderness. Lo Debar means "where nothing grows—nothingness—barren." When I think of Lo Debar, I'm reminded of pictures of our troops in the desert mountains of Afghanistan or Iraq. That is where Mephibosheth was living in shame, afraid that if he were found he'd be killed.

While I was writing this chapter, the war in Iraq was coming to an end. Baghdad had just been liberated. During the liberation, the American soldiers found a man who was on Saddam Hussein's hit list. He had been hiding out in a small basement that had been concreted over and concealed. It had a small opening where he could enter and exit. This man had lived in hiding for over twenty years! This is what Mephibosheth was doing.

In this story, Mephibosheth represents a type of you and me. And I don't know about you, but I can relate! We were born to rule and reign. We were created to be King's kids, but the Fall hit us hard. In so many ways we are crippled, living in barrenness and shame. But then along came King David, not your typical king. Neither do we serve a typical God. When tradition said kill 'em all, David called out, "Is there no one still left of the house of Saul to whom I can show God's kindness?" In that Scripture, I love the word "still." Do you know why? Because thirty years had passed since the takeover, and during his reign David had been consistently and methodically searching out people of Saul's kingdom to shower with God's grace! And he didn't give up until he found every last one.

My friend, this is what God is doing today. He's looking for people on whom He can pour out His kindness. And like Mephibosheth, all we have to do is answer the call and receive. It matters not how broken you are or how crippled you may be. It matters not if you have been living in barrenness and have nothing to offer your King. God is searching for you. He's leaving the ninety-nine sheep to seek out the one.

You may be saying to yourself, "But I am nothing. My life is nothing. I've blown it too many times." It doesn't matter.

God doesn't want what you have or what you can do. He wants *you*. Mephibosheth had nothing to offer. He wasn't a gifted speaker. He wasn't handsome. He couldn't lead. He certainly wasn't successful. He had nothing—nothing—to offer, yet David still sought him out.

Finally, when he was found, Mephibosheth thought, "This is it. I'm done for. My life is over." So he went before David and bowed before him. Yet look at David's excitement. "Mephibosheth!" he cried. David was like the Prodigal Son's father. His love for Mephibosheth was outrageous, and so is God's love for us.

Full of shame, Mephibosheth asked David, "What is your servant, that you should notice a dead dog like me?"

Has your life ever gotten so bad that you felt like a dead dog? Is that not low? Here's a guy who is born to rule and reign, and life has gotten so bad that he now sees himself as nothing more than a dead dog.

As we've seen, desperate dependence is the place where God truly becomes our source. It's also the place where we understand our total spiritual bankruptcy before God. It's when the light clicks on and we realize that no matter how much we try or how strong our willpower, we cannot live this Christian life on our own. Presented before us is the reality that if we died and stood before God, we would have nothing, absolutely nothing, but the shed blood of Christ to offer Him that could make us acceptable in His sight. We cry out along with Paul, "O wretched man I am! Who will deliver me from this body of death?"(Rom. 7:24 NKJV). This is where Mephibosheth was. He had nothing to offer, but God wanted him anyway.

True biblical humility, the kind that God blesses, is not putting yourself down. It is not being super-religious, going around saying how humble you are. It is not doing a plethora of self-denying rituals. True humility is coming to an authentic understanding of who you are before God. Until we reach that point, we cannot begin to experience the best God has to offer. I like verse thirteen: "And Mephibosheth lived in Jerusalem, because he always ate at the king's table, and he was crippled in both feet." He ate at the king's table. He took David up on his offer. He wasn't too proud. He knew he was a cripple. He understood his unworthiness. He lived with a victorious limp.

My friend, whatever transpired in your past happened. You can't undo it, but it need not conquer you. By desperately depending upon His power and grace you can move on from your past and, like Mephibosheth, you can eat from the King's table. And like Paul, you can strain toward what lies ahead. And I would like to add, it is never too late to let God take your past and begin again with Him.

A Skeptic's Transformation

Gregory Boyd's father, Edward, spent almost his entire life wavering between atheism and agnostism. An atheist says there is no God. An agnostic claims no one can know. Greg, a pastor and committed believer, began a dialogue with his father via letters with the goal of convincing him that God does, in fact, exist and Jesus is the Messiah. The letters (both son and father's) are compiled in his book *Letters from a Skeptic* (Cook, 1994).

The campaign began when Edward was seventy years old. Greg said:

> Exceptionally intelligent, intensely skeptical, very strong-willed....could a more unlikely candidate for conversion be found than my father? He had given me little grounds for hope. My father never showed any openness to the Gospel. He harbored only resentment toward the church and was outspoken in his animosity toward what he called "born-again types." The few talks about the faith he and I had had during the 14 years I had been a Christian up to the time our correspondence began had all been somewhat awkward, very short, and totally futile.[9]

After three years and thirty letters, Greg tells quite another story—a very exciting story.

While Greg was overwhelmed with joy by his father's decision to accept Christ, he wasn't very optimistic about how much transformation would take place in his post-conversion life. At seventy-three years old, his father was much older than most people who come to Christ, plus he had always been very set in his ways.

Greg's pessimism couldn't have been more misplaced. Indeed, it's difficult to exaggerate the profundity of the Holy Spirit's transformation of his father during the last eleven years of his life.

One dramatic change was in his father's emotional tenderness. The pre-Christian Ed Boyd rarely expressed his emotions—certainly not in public. But the Christian Ed Boyd became a man who wore his heart on his sleeve. Greg's father literally wept for joy every time he heard of a person coming to Christ through their correspondence—and over the course of eleven years he heard this hundreds of times!

Greg's father's faith was marked by another dramatic change. From their correspondence, it was clear faith didn't come easy for Ed. Though Ed became thoroughly convinced of the truth of the Gospel, Greg anticipated continually helping this incurable rationalist remain stable in the faith. This wasn't the case. Almost immediately after his conversion, his father seemed to rest in a profound and beautiful childlike faith.

Once, while visiting his father in a hospital after a third stroke left him nearly paralyzed, Greg told him he wanted to commission him for the most important task he could ever give someone. Since Ed was clearly going to have a lot of time on his hands as he recovered, Greg asked him to be his personal, full-time "prayer warrior." Greg explained that throughout each and every day, Ed would need to pray for him, his family, and his ministry. To Greg's surprise, his father hesitated for a moment with a concerned look on his face. Then, with very stroke-impaired speech, he asked Greg, "Do prayers that I *think* work as well as prayers that I vocalize? It's a lot of work for me to say much of anything these days."

Greg choked up at the recognition that this once arrogant intellectual giant was expressing such simple questions about God. He assured his father that God knew his thoughts without his saying them out loud. Ed gave Greg a crooked smile and muttered, "Okay then, boy, I'm your guy."

The most profound change in Greg's father's post-conversion life was his general disposition. The pre-Christian Ed Boyd was usually contentious and ill-tempered. More often than not he was angry about something and very vocal about it. Soon after his surrender to Christ, Ed Boyd acquired a profound peace, a pervasive sweetness, and—most remarkably—an amazing sense of gratitude that was never present prior to his conversion.

What made this transformation more remarkable was that, soon after he committed his life to Christ, Greg's father was given more reasons to complain than he had ever dreamed. One year after his conversion Ed suffered the first of several debilitating strokes. Over the years he lost most of his physical abilities and verbal skills. Eventually this once fiercely independent man was unable to care for himself and was confined to a wheelchair. By the age of eighty, he was almost completely blind and deaf. The pre-Christian Ed Boyd would have been positively miserable, yet the Christian Ed Boyd rarely complained.

While it sounds odd, the worse things got for Greg's father, the more grateful he became! Before his final stroke left him in a coma, Greg was with his father when he began to weep for no apparent reason. Shouting into his hearing aid, Greg requested an explanation for his tears. His response floored Greg. Sitting in his wheelchair, wearing diapers, unable to do anything but the most elementary tasks for himself, nearly totally blind and deaf, this once malcontented man said in his stroke-impaired speech, "Because I feel so blessed by God just to be here." Greg embraced his father tightly for a long moment as they both wept. Greg said, "As a witness to

the unfathomable love and power of God, this man was definitely *not* the same father grew I up with."

At the end of their visit, Greg kissed his feeble father
good-bye and said to him, "Dad, spend time dreaming about
heaven. Just enjoy imagining what it will be like." His father
smiled and simply said, "Yeah, boy." It was their last conversation. Two weeks later Ed fell into a coma from a massive
stroke that caused his brain to hemorrhage. He passed away
three weeks later.

Greg says, "One of my greatest joys is knowing my dad's
dreams of heaven have now come true. I envision him in the
presence of Christ, dancing with absolute abandon and
shouting for joy at the full realization of God's deep love for
him. I still miss him dearly, but this only makes my longing
for heaven that much sweeter."[10] If it wasn't too late for a
seventy-three-year-old agnostic, it's not too late for you.
Choose to let God free you of your haunting past, and desperately depend on Him for a joyous future.

"He does not treat us as our sins deserve or repay us
according to our iniquities.... As a father has compassion on his children, so the Lord has compassion on
those who fear him; for he knows how we are
formed, he remembers that we are dust."
—*Ps. 103:10, 13–14*

CHAPTER EIGHT

EARTHQUAKE PRAISE

"Many Christians have made the dramatic discovery of the ancient truth that we are called to praise God in all circumstances, and that miracles are often the result, the biggest of all usually being the melting of our heart."
—*Judson Cornwall*

Writing a book is difficult. It takes an incredible amount of self-discipline and grace. Contrary to what some may think, rarely do words simply leap out of your mind and onto the page. From time to time, I do get into what I call the "zone." When that happens it's a lot like surfing. You catch the wave and go with the flow. But for the most part, finding the right words, for me anyway, is a struggle—a process, like giving birth to a child. Writing a book is labor.

And writing a book like this one is not only hard labor, but it also challenges and stretches you as a person. It's my experience as a writer that by the time I put the final period on the final sentence of a book, I am a completely different person than when I began. I start the process with a goal to write a book for you, the reader, but God uses it to teach and nurture me.

Darkness Descends

After one week during the writing of this book, I found myself battling depression. Several times, my wife was moved to pray for me while she was at work, not knowing the internal battles I was going through in my office. There had been a constant flow of bad news. Five young women in our town had been brutally raped and murdered by a serial killer. As a result, Baton Rouge was getting national attention. Every time you turned on the news, there it was. At the same time, Laci Peterson and her unborn child had been found murdered in Modesto, California. The war in Iraq was raging. Each day the news would do specials on the soldiers killed in action, often dragging their grieving families before the cameras.

Then, as if that weren't enough, a string of tornadoes ravaged the Midwest leaving hundreds dead. I had just come home from an interview with Jimmy Withers, who is fathering three boys alone because his wife dropped dead from an aneurysm. On top of that, the pain I was feeling for my son's deafness was almost overwhelming.

The last straw for me came when I was watching a PBS special on television. I was enjoying the program immensely, getting caught up in the interview, when all of a sudden the sound went off. I couldn't believe it. Just as I was getting into the program, the sound went out. Now all I saw were people moving their mouths. Oh, was I frustrated! As I sat down in my chair and waited for the sound to return, it hit me like a ton of bricks, for the ten-thousandth time: *This is what it's like for my son all the time.* Waves of pain almost knocked me over and I nearly lost it.

Pain, pain, pain, everywhere I turned I was seeing pain. Then something happened. I got angry. I was really seething. Yes, I knew all the reasons why I believed God was real. I remembered all the stories and seemingly miraculous answers to prayer. I knew of God's faithfulness. In fact, I had just written a chapter on it. But none of that mattered. I was hurting and angry, to the point where I was thinking that death would be a relief.

As a result of this moment of insanity—and that's what it was, insanity—I stopped praying. It was as if I put God on hold so I could pout. Days passed. Then a week. I was sliding backward into lethargy and was hardly a fun person to be around. Yet within my anguish, I felt the tender nudging of the Holy Spirit, ever so politely calling to me. I knew I couldn't go on like this. God and I had to have a conference. I had to get back into fellowship with Him or I was going to waste away. Finally, one night when I was tossing and turning in my bed, I told my wife, Alanna, I was going to the track to pray. We live five minutes from a football field with a track around it. I go there sometimes at night to walk and pray.

Praise Me

When I got to the track I was feeling about as far from God as one could. I couldn't sense His presence. It was similar to when a husband and wife have a stand-off. You know what I'm talking about. Though they aren't saying a thing, you can cut the tension between them with a knife. Now I'm sure I was the cold one, not God, but nonetheless I didn't feel anything.

I walked around the track a couple of times and still nothing. I mean, when I tried to pray, I was shooting blanks. I came close to just giving up and going home. But as I walked, something inside my spirit said, "Praise Me." I ignored the voice and kept walking.

"Praise Me," it came again.

Inside I stiffened. I did not want to praise God.

"Praise Me."

The Spirit was unrelenting, and I knew I would never win. So after about the fourth lap, I began, with absolutely no emotion, to sing the words, "For Thou, O Lord, art high above all the earth." The words were kind of choking out of me. When I got to the words, "I exalt Thee, I exalt Thee," I forced myself to keep singing. "I exalt Thee, I exalt Thee," I continued. Then, on about the third or fourth time, the dam broke and a floodgate of praise burst from my soul. Now I was shouting! God's Spirit was washing me.

Caught up in a whirlwind of praise, the Spirit swept me along. I forgot all about my deep questions, and for nearly two hours I walked around the track unable to stop praising God. I went away charged, washed, and renewed. There were no answers. No great revelations. But God had shown up, and as I made the choice to praise Him, He triggered an earthquake in my soul. Praise works!

First Thessalonians 5:16, 18 says, "Be joyful always.... Give thanks in all circumstances, for this is God's will for you in Christ Jesus." The Bible is full of Scriptures about praise and thanksgiving. A supernatural transformation occurs when we make the choice to give thanks to God in the midst of our circumstances. God responds when, as noted in chapter 3, we choose to extol His character in the midst of crisis. And I've learned it's impossible to extol His character and grumble at the same time.

The apostle Paul said, "Rejoice in the Lord always. Again I will say, rejoice!" (Phil. 4:4 NKJV). He wasn't trying to sound religious here. When he said to rejoice in the Lord always, I think he had a pretty good idea of what "always" meant. He'd been shipwrecked, beaten several times, left for dead, abandoned by friends, and imprisoned. Plus, he had that annoying little thorn in the flesh that just wouldn't go away no matter how much he prayed. Oh yes, Paul knew pain. He knew adversity. Yet he also knew a real God, a God who never promised to keep us from suffering in this life but promised to be with us in our suffering.

The Door to Victory

Paul also knew that praise frees, that praise releases. I'm sure you remember the time Paul and his companion Silas were cast into prison. Try to picture that day. The marketplace was bustling with activity as the Middle Eastern sun of Macedonia bore down on them, amplifying the mingled smell of body odor, animals, leather, and produce. The crowd parted and formed a huge circle around Paul and Silas as they were dragged naked through the street and then flogged.

The iron pellets tied to the ends of the leather whips actually shattered bones as they landed across their backs. With each crack of the whip, the crowd cheered. Some spat upon their blood-covered bodies. Finally, when Paul and Silas lay face down in the dirt, the jailers dragged them away.

When Paul and Silas were carried away to prison, they didn't know what the future held. Paul himself had witnessed the killing of hundreds of Christians. He knew about the beheading of John the Baptist when he was in prison. They had zero reason to believe that they would ever see the light of day again. Yet what do we see? Let's read: "Again and again the rods slashed down across their bared backs; and afterwards they were thrown into prison. The jailer was threatened with death if they escaped, so he took no chances, but put them into the inner dungeon and clamped their feet into the stocks. *Around midnight, as Paul and Silas were praying and singing hymns to the Lord*—and the other prisoners were listening—suddenly there was a great earthquake; the prison was shaken to its foundations, all the doors flew open—and the chains of every prisoner fell off!" (Acts 16:23–26 TLB, emphasis added).

Earthquake praise happens when we choose to praise God smack-dab in the middle of the darkest, filthiest dungeons of life, when we are chained down, with seemingly no way out. Praise is a key that can fling open the door to victory in our lives.

When the great armies of Ammon and Moab teamed up and brought their forces against King Jehoshaphat and the people of Judah, Jehoshaphat feared that Judah would be destroyed. The armies of Ammon and Moab were far greater, both in numbers and military might. Judah could not win this battle on its own. But the Lord spoke to Jehoshaphat and told him not to fight in the battle, for the battle was not his but God's (see 2 Chron. 20:15–17).

In the midst of this crisis, facing sure destruction, as the enemy assembled its troops for battle, the men of Judah did just as God had instructed. They didn't lift a sword. Instead, they began to sing praises to the God on high.

> After consulting the people, Jehoshaphat appointed men to sing to the LORD and to praise him for the splendor of his holiness as they went out at the head of the army, saying:
>
> "Give thanks to the LORD,
> for his love endures forever."
>
> As they began to sing and praise, the LORD set ambushes against the men of Ammon and Moab and Mount Seir who were invading Judah, and they were defeated. The men of Ammon and Moab rose up against the men from Mount Seir to destroy and annihilate them. After they finished slaughtering the men from Seir, they helped to destroy one another.
> (2 Chron. 20:21–23)

Jehoshaphat and the people of Judah didn't win the battle by force, but by praise. When we praise God in the middle of our problems we allow God to take over and do battle for us.

I know all this exhortation to praise God in every circumstance can sound a bit superficial. Moreover, it can leave one with the impression that God is on an ego trip, sitting up in heaven, refusing to move until we make the "right" response. Again, it's similar to Jesus saying, "Be of good cheer." Are we really supposed to praise God when a child dies in an auto accident or when a tornado destroys one's home and takes the life of a loved one? Are we not to grieve? Yes, we are to grieve, but not "like the rest of men, who have no hope" (1 Thess. 4:13).

God is not on an ego trip. What would be ego to us is proper with God. And He is not removed from our pain. As the whip came down across Paul and Silas's backs, God the Father cringed just as Jesus wept when He received the news of Lazarus' death.

Heart Transplant

Frank Foglio's daughter was injured in an automobile accident. Her brain was severely damaged, and although many thousands of prayers were made for her recovery, her condition grew steadily worse. Finally, she had to be placed in the "hopeless" ward of an institution for the mentally ill. It was the very end of the line.

Patients in the ward were so far removed from reality that their families seldom visited. One patient had been strapped down for twelve years because of violence. Other inmates sat passively, staring at nothing, their vacant eyes reflecting brains emptied of all knowing. Still others lay rigid in beds, without sight or motion. Frank's daughter had clawed her way out of straitjackets and tried to hang herself with a bedsheet.

It had been seven years since the accident, and the absolute hopelessness of the situation began to take its toll on a very tough Italian. Frank's faith in God started to waver. On one very difficult journey to the institution, Frank was arguing with God.

"How can You be a God of love? I wouldn't permit such a thing to happen to my daughter if I had the power to prevent it. You could heal her. But You won't. Don't You love people as much as even I do? You must not." Frank felt his anger rising against God.

"Praise Me," a voice said to him.

"What for?" Frank replied.

"Praise Me that your daughter is where she is."

"Never!" he spat out. "I would rather die than do that." God had no right to ask him to praise Him when God wasn't doing His job of showing His love for people.

Frank remembered hearing a tape about giving thanks in everything. He had been deeply moved by the message, but at that moment he was in no mood to put it into practice.

"Thank Me that your daughter is exactly where she is," the voice said again.

"God, I couldn't praise You if I tried. And I'm not going to try, because I don't believe that I should."

As Frank continued toward the facility, the Holy Spirit worked in his heart, and he felt his attitude begin to soften. He said, "Well, God, I would praise You if I could, but I just can't."

A little further along, he confessed, "I would praise You, but You would have to help me."

After arriving at the institution, Frank went through the necessary procedures to get clearance to enter the most restricted part of one of the buildings. It always took a long time to get into his daughter's ward. Sometimes he wondered why he continued to come. His daughter didn't recognize him. She didn't know him from a stone on the ground.

Finally, Frank was in the last waiting room, the one that separated him from the ward. One steel door remained to be opened. Standing before it, Frank Foglio heard the calm and firm voice of God one more time: "Thank Me that your daughter is exactly where she is."

The disobedience, the unwillingness, the hardness of heart melted away. The stony heart of anger, bitterness, and unbelief somehow was replaced by a soft heart of flesh. Frank, his throat choked with emotion, whispered his surrender: "Okay, God. I thank You that my daughter is where she is. I know that You love her more than I do."

At that moment a vaguely familiar voice cried out, "I want my daddy, I want my daddy."

The attendant opened the door, and Frank raced to his daughter's compartment. Clothed in her right mind, she threw out her arms and embraced her father. Nurses, attendants, and guards gathered around and wept with joy.

Frank said, "Tell everyone our daughter is home now with us. We know that God always wants us to praise Him, regardless of how things look."[10]

In his book *Tracks of a Fellow Struggler* author John

Claypool tries to make sense of the death of his ten-year-old daughter. He concludes:

> I have two alternatives: dwelling on the fact that she has been taken away, I can dissolve in remorse that all of this is gone forever; or, focusing on the wonder that she was given to us at all, I can learn to be grateful that we shared life, even for an all-too-short ten years.... The way of remorse does not alter the stark reality one whit and only makes matters worse. *The way of gratitude does not alleviate the pain, but it somehow puts some light around the darkness and builds strength to move on.*[11]

You may be struggling with your own crisis and are nearly ready to chuck in the towel. How long have you been struggling to find an answer? How immense is your pain? God has the solution. He will release an earthquake in your soul and turn your "mourning into dancing" (Ps. 30:11 NKJV), if you will but praise Him.

"Through Jesus, therefore, let us continually
offer to God a sacrifice of praise."
—*Heb. 13:15*

CHAPTER NINE

WHAT'S IN THE WELL

> "Crises do not make you who you are.
> They reveal who you are."
> —*my grandmother*

"I'll huff and I'll puff and I'll blow your house down,"
declared the Big Bad Wolf. And that is just what he did. He
blew their houses down—at least the homes of the first two
little pigs. When the wolf came to the third house, he ran into
a slight bit of trouble. Unlike the first two pigs, the third little pig had prepared himself. Instead of building a house out
of sticks and straw, he made sure his house was constructed of
bricks and mortar and his foundation was strong. His house
was wolf-proof.

A few years ago, a series of unusually heavy thunderstorms rolled through the Atlanta area causing the Chattahoochee River to overflow its banks. The extensive flooding ruined hundreds of homes along the river. One house however, was not damaged. Although one-third of the house was underwater, not a drop came inside. The press reported it as an "architectural wonder." Just as the third little pig had designed his house with the Big Bad Wolf in mind, this house had been designed with flooding in mind.

Firm Foundations

In Matthew, Jesus said:

> Whoever hears these sayings of Mine, and does them, I will liken him to a wise man who built his house on the rock: and the rain descended, the floods came, and the winds blew and beat on that house; and it did not fall, for it was founded on the rock. But everyone who hears these sayings of Mine, and does not do them, will be like a foolish man who built his house on the sand: and the rain descended, the floods came, and the winds blew and beat on that house; and it fell. And great was its fall (Matt. 7:24–27 NKJV).

Again, consistent with His other teachings, Jesus illustrates to us that storms are going to happen, yes, even to the wise. At some point, the Big Bad Wolf is going to come knocking at our door, but we don't have to be blown away. Whether or not our house stands when the winds of adversity start blowing depends altogether on what we are made of. We may look great on the outside, but storms expose what's on the inside.

As my grandmother said, "Crises don't make you who you are. They reveal who you are." Or as someone else put it, "What's in the well comes up in the bucket." I had a professor in seminary who used to say, "You can pray and fast for an A, but if you have studied and prepared for a C, then you're going to get a C."

My father-in-law owns a bookstore, and one day he laughingly said, "Men are notorious for buying books on hunting, fishing, automobiles, and business. Then, when their marriage is falling apart, they come rushing into the store in a panic, wanting books on developing good marriages. By then, it's often too late."

Most of us are quite familiar with the above passage in Matthew. Usually when reading it, we immediately think about laying a foundation either on the rock of Christ Jesus or on the shifting sand. And that is the main thought Jesus was trying to get across. However, I would like to point out that what's interesting about building houses is that they can't be built when it's storming. Strong houses are constructed in calm, dry weather. It's during good weather that foundations are laid, houses are built, and measures are taken to ensure strength for the stormy seasons.

Likewise, it's during our good days that we build ourselves up in the faith. I once heard a pastor say, "If you can't trust God in something small, you'll never trust Him in something big." If we do not desperately depend on God and acknowledge Him in the everyday stresses of life, we will have a harder time doing it when something big hits. Merlin Carothers is the author of several best-selling books on praise. In one of his newsletters he wrote:

> We have hundreds of opportunities every day to believe God is working for our good. Every time we thank Him for something that appears to be difficult we strengthen our praise muscles. We get ready for the bigger problems that may lie ahead. But if we wait for the overwhelming problems before we begin learning, we won't be ready because we have programmed ourselves to be discouraged.
>
> When the Big One comes we will want to be able to handle it.... We win against problems and difficulties to the degree that we have prepared ourselves.[12]

When I Am Weak, Then I Am Strong

When a fierce storm hit Jimmy Withers' life suddenly one day when he was thirty-five, he was glad his faith had been built on a solid foundation, for without that foundation, he would never have made it.

After eleven years of a wonderful marriage and the birth of three active boys, Jimmy came home from work one day to find an ambulance in his front yard. At first, he thought one of the boys had been injured. Upon entering the house, he was shocked to find the paramedics doing CPR on his thirty-one-year-old, normally healthy and athletic wife, Roxanne.

He was even more shocked when she was pronounced dead at the hospital a short time later.

Devastated and bewildered, Jimmy didn't know how he was going to make it, but fourteen years later, through tears and many questions, his faith is stronger than ever. For all of those years he has been a faithful father and man of God, though he has chosen not to remarry.

As Jimmy raced to the hospital in the ambulance, it seemed like an eternity. He was thinking, "What is happening?" He kept saying over and over, "God is faithful. God is faithful." When they got to the hospital, Roxanne was wheeled to the back of the emergency room. After about thirty minutes, the doctor led Jimmy and a couple of friends into a small sitting room where the doctor said, "Roxanne suffered an aneurysm. There was nothing I could do. She's gone."

After he walked back to where Roxanne lay, Jimmy looked at her lifeless body and was overwhelmed with disbelief. "This can't be so," he thought. Later, after leaving the hospital, he cried out, "Why, God? Roxanne was so young and beautiful. Her life was just beginning. And the boys…"

As weeks went by, Jimmy struggled in deep despair—as anyone would. He saw Roxanne's clothes hanging in the closet, but he was too grief-stricken to deal with them. Finally, he asked a friend to come take her clothes, because he couldn't do it. Jimmy was paralyzed by a sense of despondency.

As weeks turned to months, the initial shock was replaced with a deep feeling of loneliness. But through the strength of friends, his parents, and other people in the body of Christ, Jimmy was able to continue on, finding strength. He also found great strength in the Word of God. One of the Scriptures that helped sustain him was 2 Corinthians 12:9 (NKJV), where God assured Paul, "My grace is sufficient for you, for My strength is made perfect in weakness."

We know that while Paul was writing this, something had afflicted him, and it's as we find our own weaknesses that we are made strong. We realize and recognize the power of Christ in that. Paul continued to say, "Therefore most gladly I will rather boast in my infirmities, that the power of Christ may rest upon me." Paul understood this concept so well that he looked forward to infirmities because he knew that then the power of Christ would be realized. He said, "Therefore I take pleasure in infirmities, in reproaches, in needs, in persecutions, in distresses, for Christ's sake. For when I am weak, then I am strong" (2 Cor. 12:10 NKJV) .

Those verses have become very real to Jimmy through the years, during times of weakness, despondency, despair, and periods of strong temptation. Jimmy said, "I've found that in my weakness, Christ would come to me."

But like everyone, there were moments when Jimmy felt God's silence. Once he told God, "Lord, You promised I would never thirst again." He said, "There were times when I went through life very mechanically and didn't understand God's silence."

Two other passages of Scripture that helped sustain Jimmy were Romans 8:18 and 2 Corinthians 4:17: "For I consider that the sufferings of this present time are not worthy to be compared with the glory which shall be revealed in us" (Rom. 8:18 NKJV). "For our light affliction, which is but for a moment, is working for us a far more exceeding and eternal weight of glory" (2 Cor. 4:17 NKJV).

Jimmy said, "Those Scriptures become all sustaining when we recognize that God's power is sufficient. If we had not been asked to walk through the darkness of night, we would not know the sufficiency and depth of His grace. Many times through the years I've felt God's silence and I've wondered what purpose it serves. Though I still miss Roxanne so much, without her loss I couldn't know Christ's sufficiency in such a meaningful way. I take comfort knowing that my sweet wife is in His incredible presence and that I'll see her soon."

Jimmy has looked his opponent square in the eyes and has not run. Yes, he has experienced great grief. Sorrow and temptation he knows well. He's felt the noose of discouragement pulled tightly around his neck. And he absorbs the blows of loneliness. But Jimmy is winning by the power of Christ. God's grace and strength have become his closest allies.

Jimmy said, "God has put within our lives pain to remind us of our dependency upon Him and scars to always recognize that there is a healing process and that I am dependent upon Him. We have to be cognizant that God's sufficiency is there in the midst of our pain."

Jimmy's story reminds me of Proverbs 10:25: "When the storm has swept by, the wicked are gone, but the righteous stand firm forever." The storm has raged in Jimmy's life, yet he has stood strong for over fourteen years. His faith has not endured by accident, but because he has built a strong house with a solid foundation.

In his story several things leap out as bricks, beams, and bedrock in his house. Before we review them, however, I would like to point out that the foundational elements in a strong house are usually the most basic elements, nonetheless they are the most important.

Basic Training

Growing up, I was pretty athletic, particularly in football. I played every year from the third grade and was fortunate to get a scholarship to the University of Mississippi. After that, I had a short-lived tryout at a pro minicamp. One of the things that amazed me about college and professional football is that at every practice, we always spent a certain amount of time on the fundamentals of the game—the very same fundamentals that I worked on in elementary school. The running backs would practice holding the football in a way that would prevent fumbling. The receivers would work on "looking" the ball into their hands—not running before the ball is caught. The defensive players would work on form tackling and locking up their opponents. The offensive line would practice blocking. We would work on these basics, sometimes for an hour, before we ever worked on running plays or reviewing the opponent. Though the basics are sometimes routine in our lives, they are the foundation of everything we build upon. The apostle Peter said, "I will always remind you of these things, even though you know them and are firmly established in the truth you now have. I think it is right to refresh your memory as long as I live in the tent of this body" (2 Peter 1:12–13).

Peter's words sound a lot like my football coaches! He knew the importance of practicing the fundamentals even though his readers already knew them and were firmly established. Just because we are firmly established doesn't mean we can afford to stop the basics. Just because I made it to the collegiate level in football didn't mean I could stop practicing the basics. My college coach used to stress that nine times out of ten, a game was won or lost not because the other team was that much better, but because of a breakdown in the fundamentals. This principle is true in sports, relationships, building houses, and business. It's a universal truth.

Jimmy Withers was established in the basics. The fundamentals carried him through his incredible storm. The following three elements made his house strong.

1. *Jimmy had a relationship with God.* I can almost hear you now. Of course we need a relationship with God. Man, this really *is* basic. The truth is, however, many people are Christians and are trusting Jesus for their salvation, but they don't have a real relationship with God. If they treated their spouse the way they do God, they would be divorced in a heartbeat. Could you imagine if you spoke to your spouse only a couple of times a week, if that? And when you did, it was in a very formal, systematic way, half the time just asking him or her for something? God doesn't want our religious formalities. He wants us. He wants sons and daughters and friends. And when you really get to know Him in the everyday routine of life, you will know Him in the storm.

When Jesus instructed His disciples to pray, He told them to begin by praying, "Our Father in heaven" (Matt. 6:9). The word Jesus used for "Father" is the Aramaic term *Abba*. This is a word—like Daddy or Papa—that small children once used for their fathers. Jesus was stressing an intimate way of addressing God. By calling God Abba, He was suggesting a relationship of the deepest intimacy. When my children call me Daddy, they are using that name with all its privileges. "Daddy" means they can approach me. They can hop onto my lap. They can ride on my back. They can call out for me at night when they are scared. This is what Jesus was trying to get across.

Do you know God like that? Hebrews 4:16 (NKJV) encourages us to "come boldly to the throne of grace, that we may obtain mercy and find grace to help in time of need". To me this further illustrates a deep, personal relationship. Thinking about this Scripture, I picture myself boldly entering my parents' home anytime I want. When I go to their house I feel a certain confidence to raid the refrigerator or just make myself comfortable. I don't have to ask. It's my folks' house, therefore it's my house.

This how God wants us to know Him—not disrespectfully, yet with the confidence that we are family. Having a relationship with God like this is a vital building block in a solid house. With a relationship like this with God, though we are sometimes isolated, we will never be alone. When Daniel was in the lions' den, he was secluded and it was dark, and he could feel the lions' breath bearing down upon him. Yet he knew he wasn't alone, that Abba was right there with him.

2. *Jimmy was established in the Word of God.* Jimmy pointed out that certain Scriptures were a comfort to him. He was able to lean upon them in the storm because he had planted them in his mind well before the storm hit. When we meditate and learn Scriptures, the Holy Spirit will bring them to our mind in times of crisis.

The psalmist meditated daily on the principles of God. "But his delight is in the law of the LORD, and on his law he meditates day and night. He is like a tree planted by streams of water, which yields its fruit in season and whose leaf does not wither" (Ps. 1:2–3). To meditate means to ponder and reflect upon something over and over until it becomes a part of you. Let us not be fooled—meditating on Scripture, though basic, is one of the most life-sustaining acts we can do.

When Paul was in prison for the last time, he knew his work was finished and he sensed death was imminent. As he sat in that cold dungeon, lonely and forsaken by most, he sent a message to Timothy asking him to bring some supplies. Paul wrote, "When you come, bring the cloak that I left with Carpus at Troas, and my scrolls, especially the parchments" (2 Tim. 4:13). Paul stressed that he wanted the parchments, which were the Scriptures. He knew that in his darkest hour he needed not the writings of other men but the writings of God.

While reading other books is a good thing, they can never replace filling our minds with the Word of God. Something supernatural happens when we meditate upon Scripture. We become transformed. And in times of crisis, the Holy Spirit will bring those words to our minds for strength and encouragement.

3. Jimmy was connected with his family, the body of Christ.
We may want to be loners because Christians and the so-called church have let us down. Here's a quick word of exhortation: Get over it! And don't go looking for a perfect church, because you will ruin it! The bottom line is this: We all fail. We all fall short. We all are imperfect humans and we all need each other. And despite what you've heard, the body of Christ does respond in times of crises. I've seen it many times.

Of course, we must learn to discern the true body of Christ from the "institutional church," which is the building and all the programs that go along with it. An institution may or may not represent the true church, the body of Christ. The true church is about relationships. The Bible says, "For where two or three come together in my name, there am I with them" (Matt. 18:20). Some of the most powerful church services I've been a part of were between another person and myself. I've seen God do incredible things as I was sharing a meal with someone.

We must develop godly relationships during the calm times of our lives, and those people *will* be a source of strength when storms hit. The true church is made of people God has brought into our lives who support and live in covenant with us. You can have church at lunch with someone or on a walk or at a place of worship. The church is flexible, but developing relationships is not optional for solid growth.

Personally, at different stages of my life, God has brought to me godly friends who have encouraged me in my walk with Christ. When I went through my divorce, I would like to say that the institutional church did a lot for me. But the truth is, it didn't. Yet God sent me godly people at strategic times who carried me when I couldn't stand. They opened their homes, gave me money, counseled me, laughed with me, encouraged me, listened to me, and prayed with me. Jimmy also had those people and they helped him through. Now don't get me wrong. I believe in the institutional church; I go to one every Sunday. Yet as I grow in my faith I'm seeing that long-term growth happens when we are connected via relationships to one another and that connection is a lifeline when storms hit.

Three Myths That Destroy Foundations

1. I don't have time to study God's Word or pray.

God's answer: "Be diligent to present yourself approved to God, a worker who does not need to be ashamed, rightly dividing the word of truth" (2 Tim. 2:15 NKJV).

2. I love God, but I don't need the church because of all the hypocrites.

God's answer: "Let us not give up meeting together, as some are in the habit of doing, but let us encourage one another—and all the more as you see the Day approaching" (Heb. 10:25).

3. I just don't feel anything when I pray or spend time with God.

God's answer: "Ask, and you will be given what you ask for. Seek, and you will find. Knock, and the door will be opened. For everyone who asks, receives. Anyone who seeks, finds. If only you will knock, the door will open" (Matt. 7:7–8 TLB).

It's never too late to begin building a house with a solid foundation. To do so, you may have to tear down some old walls, maybe demolish your existing house and build anew. If you do, it will be worth it, and when the Big Bad Wolf comes to your door, you will be ready.

> "Above all else, guard your heart,
> for it is the wellspring of life."
> —*Solomon (Prov. 4:23)*

CHAPTER TEN

THORNS OF GRACE

"Where there is sorrow, there is holy ground."
—*Oscar Wilde*

The apostle Paul's life was overflowing with confirmation of God's supernatural love and power. Many people who came to him were dramatically healed. Thousands were converted. In the city of Lystra he had been instrumental in the healing of a man who had been a paralytic from birth. In addition to his dramatic Damascus road conversion, Paul had many dreams and visions. A man appeared to him in a vision one night begging him to come over to Macedonia (see Acts 16:9). As a result, Paul changed his course. Talk about direction!

Once he was taken up to heaven. Some scholars believe Paul had a near-death experience during one of the times he was left for dead. Personally, I can't make that determination, but the Scripture says,

> I know a man in Christ who fourteen years ago was caught up to the third heaven. Whether it was in the body or out of the body I do not know—God knows. And I know that this man—whether in the body or apart from the body I do not know, but God knows—was caught up to paradise. He heard inexpressible things, things that man is not permitted to tell. (2 Cor. 12:2–4)

That We Might Not Rely on Ourselves

Paul indeed experienced remarkable success. He was responsible for writing much of the New Testament and evangelizing most of the then-civilized world. Yet, as we have noted, he also endured much suffering.

> I have...been in prison more frequently, been flogged more severely, and been exposed to death again and again. Five times I received from the Jews the forty lashes minus one. Three times I was beaten with rods, once I was stoned, three times I was shipwrecked, I spent a night and a day in the open sea, I have been constantly on the move. I have been in danger from rivers, in danger from bandits, in danger from my own countrymen, in danger from Gentiles; in danger in the

city ... in danger from false brothers. I have labored and
toiled and have often gone without sleep; I have known
hunger and thirst and have often gone without food; I
have been cold and naked. (2 Cor. 11:23–27)

A friend of mine who travels and speaks all over the world
told me once, "He who is used greatly must suffer deeply." I
have never forgotten his words, and they were true for the
apostle Paul. Paul suffered greatly but was used deeply.
However, it was also Paul who wrote so movingly of God's
goodness.

For I am convinced that neither death nor life, neither angels nor demons, neither the present nor the
future, nor any powers, neither height nor depth, nor
anything else in all creation, will be able to separate us
from the love of God that is in Christ Jesus our Lord.
(Rom. 8:38–39)

Paul stayed confident because he understood the role of
suffering in his life. In 2 Corinthians 1:8–9 Paul makes an
incredible statement—a statement that is really the foundation of this whole book. "We were under great pressure, far
beyond our ability to endure, so that we despaired even of
life. Indeed, in our hearts we felt the sentence of death. *But
this happened that we might not rely on ourselves but on God,
who raises the dead*" (emphasis added).

Wow! Did you get that? All of this bad stuff happened that
"we might not rely on ourselves but on God, who raises the

dead." That's it. Paul nailed it in just a few words. Let me ask you this: Have you ever been under such pressure, far beyond your ability to endure? I sure have. In your heart, have you ever felt the sentence of death? I sure have. You know what I'm talking about. You feel so much pressure that death seems easier than living another day. Well, Paul declares that this happens so we will rely on God and not ourselves. God wants us to be desperately dependent upon Him.

I happened to talk with a woman while I was writing this book. She asked me the title. When I told her it was *Desperate Dependence,* she said, "Have I got a story for you." Then she proceeded to tell me her story of desperate dependence. But one thing she said really stuck with me. She said, "You know, God will take you to the very edge of the cliff where, if you take one more step, you will plummet to your death, but that is right where He wants us, so we will depend upon Him."

Paul knew this. He understood that the Christian life is a life lived with divine tension. As long as we are in this flesh there will always be evil, suffering, and a tension between what we are and what we desire to be. Ultimate fulfillment will never happen in this life.

> Therefore we do not lose heart. Though outwardly we are wasting away, yet inwardly we are being renewed day by day. For our light and momentary troubles are achieving for us an eternal glory that far outweighs them all. So we fix our eyes not on what is seen, but on what is unseen. For what is seen is temporary, but what

is unseen is eternal.... Meanwhile we groan, longing to be clothed with our heavenly dwelling.... For while we are in this tent [body], we groan and are burdened. (2 Cor. 4:16–18; 5:2, 4)

What I've come to understand is that suffering helps bring eternity into focus. And this is not a depressing or negative thing. It gives us a proper perspective. Some people have said, "I don't want to be so heavenly minded that I'm no earthly good." While that sounds good, it is not scriptural. This life is only temporary. It is "a mist that appears for a little while and then vanishes"(James 4:14). The closer we get to God, the less this world and the things in it mean to us. And suffering helps remind us of that.

Things to Do

I remember vividly when I was in seminary and first began the ministry. I'd hear some dear saint talking about how he or she longed for heaven or Jesus' soon return and though I'd say "amen," deep in my heart I just didn't get it. It wasn't that I didn't love Jesus, but I had things I wanted to do. I wanted to build that house in the country and raise up a successful church and write books and have kids. Even though I wanted Jesus to come back, I really wanted Him to wait a while. The above Scriptures about groaning and longing didn't mean much to me because, in all honesty, I really loved this life.

Then something happened. Suffering happened. Pain happened. And with each trial the things of this world became just a little bit less important. Heaven looked better all the time. What began to matter more and more to me was finding comfort and rest in His presence—living in His presence and loving people. Suffering caused me to come to grips with death. Now death doesn't scare or even bother me anymore. Truly, I look forward to being with my Lord.

I do groan and long for eternity. That's one reason I can look back on my own suffering and actually thank God. Because coming to this point has not been a negative experience, but a freeing one. When death and the things of this world no longer hold their power over you, then you are truly free to live. John Erskine, an eminent Scottish theologian, once said, "He who fears death has missed the point of life." I would say, "He who loves this life and the things of this world is not free to live." When I say love, I do not mean enjoy. God wants us to enjoy life, but we are truly free to do that when we understand that ultimate fulfillment will not happen here—that nothing, absolutely nothing other than God, can satisfy. It's at that point God can release us to have things, because the things won't have us. There is a big difference.

Suffering and trials help bring us to this point, and the apostle Paul was aware of it. He knew that God never wants us to lapse into casual comfort but to seek after Him desperately and make Him the focal point of our lives. That's why Paul could write so confidently, "I delight in weakness, in insults, in hardships, in persecutions, in difficulties. For when I am weak, then I am strong" (2 Cor. 12:10).

Living with Thorns

Most of us are familiar with Paul's famous "thorn in the flesh." Though he begged and prayed to God on three different occasions to remove it, God refused, replying, "My grace is sufficient for you, for my power is made perfect in weakness" (2 Cor. 12:9).

Though what the thorn was has been debated, one thing we are certain of is that it caused Paul great distress, and God allowed it. God wanted Paul to desperately depend on Him for daily provisions. God allowed Paul to live with that thorn, in constant tension, in order that Christ's power would be evident in his life.

Just as God allowed Paul's thorn to remain, causing constant tension, so God allows them to remain in our lives also. When these thorns persist, they prick us, causing us to live in that place of tension. But if we could look into the future we would see that they, in reality, are a tremendous blessing from God causing us to desperately depend upon Him. If we will but let them, they can become "thorns of grace" exposing our weaknesses so we can experience God's power and truly live.

> "Therefore I will boast all the more
> gladly about my weaknesses, so that
> Christ's power may rest on me."
> —*Paul (2 Cor. 12:9)*

CHAPTER ELEVEN

GOD STILL DOES MIRACLES

"The miracles of Christianity are not an embarrassment to the Christian worldview. Rather, they are testimony to the compassion of God for human beings benighted by sin and circumstance."
—*Gary Habermas*

At this point, it's extremely important to say that it isn't my intention to be the bearer of doom and gloom. While life is difficult and trials are a normal part of the human experience, I am not advocating that we take on a storm mentality—living our lives as if life is nothing but pain. The good thing about storms is that they always pass.

In chapter 3 we discussed the two sides of God's faithfulness—His faithfulness to supernaturally deliver and His faithfulness to walk with us through fire. Both require our faith. Thus far we've focused pretty much on desperately depending on God to take us through the fire and storms. But in all fairness, we must focus on both sides, not just one.

Yes, King David did proclaim God's faithfulness when he didn't see an answer. He knew what it was like to feel the absence of God when he cried out, "I am worn out calling for help; my throat is parched. My eyes fail, looking for my God" (Ps. 69:3). But on the other hand, David did see God move in mighty ways to deliver him. Yes, he felt God's silence at times, but he did slay Goliath and declared, "I will praise you, O LORD, with all my heart; I will tell of all your wonders" (Ps. 9:1). What wonders was David talking about? He was talking about all the times God delivered him and his people.

Abraham and Sarah had to wait until they had lost all hope of having a child, but God did deliver Isaac in His own time. Joseph was in prison for over a decade, but God did deliver him. Jesus showed up in the storm, and the storm ceased. When Peter was drowning he cried out in desperation, "Lord, save me!" Yet, Peter did walk on water. And as far as we know, he is the only person in history other than Christ to do so. God is a God of supernatural deliverance, and it is our right and responsibility to cry out to Him and expect Him to act. "Oh my soul, don't be discouraged. Don't be upset. Expect God to act!... He is my help! He is my God!" (Ps. 42:11 TLB).

Hebrews 11:6 says, "And without faith it is impossible to please God, because anyone who comes to him must believe that he exists and that he rewards those who earnestly seek him." God is not an impersonal force behind the cosmos. He is the God of creation—the God of the universe. And that same God of the universe is a very personal God; He knows specifically where you are, and He wants to deliver you or give you the strength and peace needed to stand.

A Skeptic's Declaration

I want to talk in this chapter about God's supernatural answers to prayer and miracles. We serve a God who is very much alive today and is involved personally in our lives. He is a God who still does supernatural signs and wonders.

Before I go any further, however, it is necessary that I show you my character and what I stand for. I gave my life to Christ when I was seventeen. I've been to seminary. I've led Bible studies, pastored a congregation, preached in countless churches, performed weddings for Christian couples, done funerals, and I am a skeptic. Yes, I'm a skeptic. In times past my skepticism has entertained thoughts of agnosticism and for fleeting moments, even atheism. I must admit that I have struggled with doubt. Sometimes serious, overwhelming, complicated doubt. Call it a lack of faith. Call it weakness. Call it what you will. But I, like the father of the boy possessed by an evil spirit, have cried out, "Lord, help me in my unbelief." And over time, God has answered my heart's cry. It's as if my unbiased skepticism was actually driving me to the truth. I tell young people today, Don't be afraid to ask tough questions or to examine both sides of the issues. However, when you do, make sure that you do it with no biases. When you honestly seek truth, the truth will always prevail.

Since my undergraduate days, a passion has gripped my inner man to know truth—not just what a preacher says—but truth. Today I am completely convinced that Jesus Christ is truth, the Bible is the Word of God, and that God knows us intimately. I believe that from both personal experience and sound reason. For over twenty years I've studied apologetics (the defense of the Christian faith). In addition to reading and listening to the world's leading scientists and theologians, I have investigated and researched testimonies of God's miraculous intervention.

What I've come to see is that there are many indisputable evidences for God's existence—and not only that He exists, but that He is most definitely personally involved in our lives. We will talk about some of the scientific evidences in the next chapter, but in this chapter I want to focus on testimonies of God's supernatural answers to prayer in modern times.

As a skeptic, it is important to note that while I am enthusiastic about my faith, I hate misinformation and embellishment. I am acutely aware that Christians many times tend to get caught up in the emotion of telling a story and stretch the facts; sometimes they outright lie. This does not diminish the fact, however, that literally thousands of credible, well-documented testimonies are simply inexplicable unless God miraculously intervened. To tell you how skeptical I am, many times, if I read an incredible claim, I will actually find the person involved and call him or her to verify the account.

Another important thing I must point out is that miracles don't always happen. I've seen many faithful men and women of God suffer without receiving a miracle. Remember, I have a deaf son for whom I would gladly give up my hearing. I've prayed years for a miracle. It hasn't happened. Yet I firmly believe God does do miracles today, and we are supposed to ask Him. However, we are not to seek after miracles for miracles' sake. Rather, we are to seek a relationship with God. Miracles are an act of His absolute sovereignty. When using the term *miracle* in this chapter, I simply mean an event that is not only highly improbable, but there is no apparent explanation for the occurrence apart from a supernatural intervention.

The following are true stories from extremely credible sources. Over the years I've researched and collected hundreds of accounts. Also, in my own life, I've experienced several astonishing supernatural events. As you read about those, know that I took great pains to tell the events exactly as they occurred. What you do with these stories is your own business. However, if they are true, then we must take their message seriously. The message: God is alive and He knows exactly where we are. He is in the midst of the storm with us whether or not He chooses to deliver us.

The Holy Spirit Reveals a Secret

It was the end of a long day of ministry, and John Wimber was exhausted. John was the pastor and founder of Vineyard Christian Fellowship in California, which started as a home prayer meeting and has since mushroomed into hundreds of congregations with over 100,000 members. He had just completed a teaching conference in Chicago and was flying off to another speaking engagement in New York. John was looking forward to the plane ride as a chance to relax for a few hours before plunging back into teaching. But it was not to be the quiet, uneventful trip he had hoped for.

Shortly after takeoff, he pushed back the reclining seat and adjusted the seat belt, preparing to relax. As he did, his eyes wandered around the cabin, not looking at anything in particular. Seated across the aisle from him was a middle-aged businessman—nothing unusual or noteworthy about him. But in the split second that John's eyes happened to be cast in his direction, he saw something that startled him.

Written across the businessman's face in very clear and distinct letters John thought he saw the word "adultery." He blinked, rubbed his eyes, and looked again. But it was still there. "Adultery." John said, "I was seeing it not with my eyes, but in my mind's eye. No one else on the plane, I am sure, saw it." It was the Spirit of God communicating to him. The fact that it was a spiritual phenomenon made it no less real.

By now the businessman had become aware that John was looking at him ("gaping at him" might be a more accurate description).

"What do you want?" he snapped at John.

As he spoke, a woman's name came clearly to John's mind. Somewhat nervously, John leaned across the aisle and asked, "Does the name Jane (not her real name) mean anything to you?"

The businessman's face turned ashen. "We've got to talk," he stammered.

The plane was a jumbo jet, the kind with a small upstairs cocktail lounge. John followed the businessman up the stairs to the lounge. As they did, John sensed the Spirit speaking to him yet again. "Tell him if he doesn't turn from his adultery, I'm going to take him."

"Terrific," John thought. "All I wanted was a nice, peaceful plane ride to New York. Now here I was, sitting in an airplane cocktail lounge with a man I had never seen before, whose name I didn't even know, about to tell him God was going to take his life if he didn't stop his affair with some woman."

The two sat down in strained silence. The businessman looked at John suspiciously for a moment, then asked, "Who told you that name?"

"God told me," John blurted out.

"God told you?" the man almost shouted the question.

"Yes," John answered, taking a deep breath. "He also told me to tell you…that unless you turn from this adulterous relationship, He is going to take your life."

John braced for an angry, defensive reaction, but to his relief the businessman's defensiveness crumbled and his heart melted. In a choked, desperate voice he asked John, "What should I do?"

At last John was back on familiar ground and explained to him what it meant to repent and trust Christ, and invited him to pray with him. With hands folded and head bowed, John began to lead him in a quiet prayer. "O God…"

That was as far as they got. The conviction of sin that had

built up inside the man seemed virtually to explode. Bursting into tears, he cried out, "Oh, God, I'm so sorry" and launched into a heartrending repentance.

It was impossible, in such cramped quarters, to keep hidden what was happening. Before long everyone in the cocktail lounge was acquainted with this man's past sinfulness and present contrition. The flight attendants were even weeping right along with him.

When they finished praying and the man regained his composure, the two talked for a while about what had happened to him.

"The reason I was so upset when you first mentioned that name to me," he explained, "was that my wife was sitting in the seat right next to me. I didn't want her to hear."

"You're going to have to tell her," John replied.

"I am?" he responded weakly. "When?"

"Better do it right now."

The prospect of confessing to his wife was, understandably, somewhat intimidating, but he could see there was no other way. So the two headed down the stairs and back to their seats.

John couldn't hear the conversation over the noise of the plane, but he could see the wife's stunned reaction, not only to the man's confession of infidelity, but also to his account of how the stranger sitting across the aisle had been sent by God to warn him of the consequences of his sin. Eyes wide with amazement, she stared first at her husband, then at John, then back at her husband, then back at John, as the amazing story unfolded. In the end the man led his wife to accept Christ, right there on the airplane.

There was little time to talk when they got off the airplane in New York. They didn't own a Bible, so John gave them his. Then they went their separate ways.[13]

A Blind Woman Receives Her Sight

As a young woman, Marolyn Ford began to lose her eyesight. It progressively got worse and worse. The doctor told her she had an irreversible problem called macular degeneration. He predicted that it would progress until she would be legally blind. This indeed happened. She lost her sight and had to go to a school for the blind to learn to use a cane and to read Braille.

But the story does not end there. When Marolyn attended Bible college the professors allowed her to take classes with a tape recorder. There, as a sightless young girl, she met a young ministerial student named Acie Ford. They fell in love, and this young preacher married a bride who was beautiful but could not see her bridegroom.

God gave them a little baby. She could not see the face of her baby, either. God gave them a wonderful church, and she knew her church members by voice but could not see their faces.

Marolyn had prayed many times that she might be healed by miracle or medicine, but nothing seemed to help. One evening after a time of ministry, she and her husband were driving home late at night. They discussed Marolyn's blindness. Acie talked to her about the impediment it was to the ministry and how wonderful it would be if God would heal her. In her book, *These Blind Eyes Now See,* Marolyn says that on one particular evening, when both of them were exhausted, Acie picked up a religious periodical, and she climbed into bed. After reading for a minute, Acie put the magazine down, got on his knees for his nightly devotion, and began praying.

They both began to cry as he prayed with great feeling and boldness: "Oh, God! You can restore Marolyn's eyesight tonight, Lord. I know you can do it! And, God, if it be Your will, I pray You will do it tonight." Neither of them was quite prepared for what happened. After twelve blurred and dark years, there was sharpness and light.

"Acie, I can see!" Marolyn exclaimed.

"You're kidding," he answered.

"I can see! I can see the pupils in your eyes!" she repeated.

Acie thought that perhaps just a little vision had come back.

"Acie, it's 12:30 at night," Marolyn said. "You need a shave! I can see!"

Acie still couldn't believe the miracle that had really occurred. He grabbed a newspaper, pointed to the large print at the top of the page, and asked, "Can you see this?"

"I can do better than that!" she exclaimed. "I can read the smaller print!"

Acie got excited. "Marolyn, can you see the dresser? Can you see the bed?"

They shouted and praised the Lord for what He had done. Such a miracle was overwhelming. Things had been rough for Acie as he tried to keep up with both his church work and his sales job. He had nearly reached his limit that evening when the miracle happened. Both of them believed that God was able, yet they had a hard time comprehending that something so wonderful and miraculous had happened to them.

Jumping off the bed, Acie asked the question again, "Marolyn, can you see?"

"Yes!"

"Praise God! Praise God! Praise God! Glory, glory, glory to God! It can't be!" Acie exclaimed.

The couple were beside themselves with happiness. "This is heaven!" Acie shouted. "It has to be! Oh, God, why did I doubt You?"

Then he turned to Marolyn. "Why did I doubt God? I didn't believe He could do something like this! He did it!"

Psalm 116:12 (KJV)—"What shall I render unto the LORD for all his benefits toward me?"—came to Acie's mind. The two were jumping up and down and crying at the same time. Marolyn was getting her first look at her husband. For the first time, she could see his face, his eyes, his nose, his mouth. She could see!

Marolyn ran to look in the mirror and could hardly believe how her facial features had changed. She had become blind at nineteen; now she was thirty-one. Over and over, she kept glancing in the mirror.

Too excited to contain themselves, they called Marolyn's parents. When the phone rang at her parents' home in Michigan, her mother was awake—she had not been able to sleep that night. For years she had been burdened with the thought of her daughter's blindness and her own helplessness in not being able to do anything about it. How happy the news made her! She rejoiced with Marolyn and Acie over the telephone lines. Marolyn asked her mother to share the news with the others in her family who lived in Michigan and with her twin sister in New York.

Then Acie dialed his parents, and his mother sleepily answered. Acie shouted, "Mother, Marolyn can see!"

Acie's mother been awakened in the middle of the night by a son too excited to speak calmly. "Is everything all right?" she asked.

All Acie could do was repeat over and over, "Marolyn can see! Marolyn can see! She can see!"

They wanted to run down the street at 1 A.M. and shout that Marolyn was blind, but now she could see!

The director of the school for the blind said she should go to the doctor and let him confirm this miracle.

The doctor who had examined her before in her blindness put the eye charts in front of her. She read them with ease. He said to her, "I cannot doubt or deny that you can see. Now let me look into your eyes."

When he did, he gasped. He said, "I don't understand it. There is really no change. A portion of your eyes is like a mirror that has had the quicksilver scraped off." He said it was a bigger miracle than he would have believed. "It is impossible for you to see and yet you see."

In the years since then, Marolyn has crossed America giving her testimony. It has blessed and strengthened thousands. She does not believe it is always God's will to heal, but she cannot deny what God has done for her.[14]

The Guitar

While studying journalism at the University of Mississippi, I experienced an extraordinary event that I could not dismiss as mere coincidence. One night, during the Christmas break,

I began my regular prayer routine. As I prayed, something happened in my inner mind. It's hard to explain, but a voice, a still small voice, permeated my inner mind saying, "Give your guitar away." At that time, I was interested in playing the guitar and singing. So this was not something I wanted to hear or do. I didn't have much money, and giving away a two hundred-dollar guitar would mean I would be without one for the foreseeable future.

I went to bed trying to dismiss this thought, but the more I wished it away, the stronger it became. Eventually, I fell asleep. When I picked up my guitar the next morning, boom, the thought came back. For days, every time I picked up my guitar, that thought nagged me. It just wouldn't leave me alone. Finally, I said, "Okay, God, you win. I'll give my guitar away." As soon as I said that, a name popped into my head—John Edwards. I was puzzled because I knew that John, who attended a Bible study with me, did not play the guitar.

John had gone home for the holidays, so I would have to wait a couple of weeks to see him, but my mind was resolved. John was getting the guitar. When classes resumed after the break, I met with John and said to him, "John, you may think I'm crazy, but God wants me to give you this guitar. If you don't play, keep it anyway." I was expecting John to look at me as if I had lost my mind, but to my surprise, tears filled his eyes. Then, right there, on the spot, he pulled out of his book bag a journal and told me that over the holidays, while in prayer, God had spoken to him as well and told him to write down the following words. As long as I live, I will never forget those words. I can quote them to this day, because I've reflected on them many times. "There is a guitar, which I, the Lord God, am going to give you. Though you do not know how to play, I will teach you to play and sing praises to Me."

John believed that if the inner voice that compelled him to write those words was God's then somehow God would provide him a guitar. Then, without any knowledge of what John had written, I sought him out and gave him my guitar that I didn't even want to give away! Both John and I were amazed. Neither of us understood why God had done what He did, but we absolutely knew He was real and personally involved in our lives.

Why I Write Fiction

After I finished writing my second nonfiction book, *It's Only a Flat Tire in the Rain*, I started praying about what to write next. One evening, while walking and praying on our land, an unexpected thought popped into my mind—very similar to the thought about giving my guitar away. Over the years, I've come to know that voice as the Holy Spirit, but I always like to test it first. I believe that if a thought is of God, He will confirm it. Anyway, the thought that came to me was this: "I want you to start writing fiction. Though you are a good speaker, you can be a great writer. Fiction can be a strong evangelism tool because we live in an age when people respond to stories."

I must say that this thought surprised me. When I went out to pray, I was thinking about my next nonfiction book and a career as a speaker. You see, that is where I was having success—I'd had two books published by two of the top New York houses, Putnam and Bantam Doubleday. Why change and write fiction? Though I had toyed with it, I was a novice at fiction writing. The message just didn't make sense. So, as I did with the guitar thought, I brushed it aside and moved on. But the thought hounded me—tormented me would be a more realistic description. Every time I sat down at my computer to start my next nonfiction work, I would freeze. It was as if God were saying, "You're not obeying Me." Yet when I fiddled around with fiction, I felt a strange peace.

It was May 2000 and *Flat Tire* wasn't scheduled to hit the stores until January 2001. Now was the time to start on my next work. As a writer, you always want to have something in the pipeline. A month passed and I was still vacillating with this thought hounding me. On Saturday, June 17, 2000, I prayed for God to confirm to me if this persistent voice was from Him.

The next day at church my pastor preached a sermon using the movie *Chariots of Fire* as an illustration. In the movie, Eric Liddell, an Olympic runner and later a missionary to China, was asked, "Why bother with running if you are called to China?" Eric answered, "God made me fast and when I run I feel His pleasure."

When my pastor quoted those words, I felt the presence of God wash over me. That was exactly how I felt when I wrote and thought about fiction. I didn't understand what God was doing, but I felt His pleasure when I did it. My pastor went on to say that God wants to give His people creative talents that pierce the culture with His worldview. I knew the sermon was for me, and I wrote the Liddell quote in my journal. My wife had not gone to church that day, and when I got home I enthusiastically shared with her that I felt God had confirmed His word to me. It was settled in my heart. I would pursue fiction even if it didn't make sense. I told my agent, who I'm pretty sure thought I was crazy, and I began writing fiction.

After putting my nonfiction aside and writing fiction for two months, I received a letter from Mark Victor Hansen, the author of *Chicken Soup for the Soul.* The letter announced that he would be endorsing the cover of my upcoming book! This was a big deal. The Chicken Soup series has sold over 200 million copies, and the authors receive thousands of requests for endorsements. The fact that they picked my book was a very big deal. My publisher and my agent went nuts. I went nuts. Everyone was telling me, "You have to do nonfiction. That is where all your success is going to be." So, caught up in all the hoopla, I put the fiction aside and again started on my next nonfiction book—without consulting God.

Guess what? When I sat down to write, I got the same feelings as before. It was as if God had taken His hand off my nonfiction work. It was a terrible feeling and I was confused. I know you may be saying to yourself, "Why can't he just do both?" I do both, but for some reason God was trying to get my attention to start seriously pursuing fiction.

You see, fiction is a whole different ball game. If you are to be successful it requires focus. Adding fiction to my career would be like a plumber deciding to add electrical work to his job title. It takes a lot of training and development. And I was already having success with what I was doing.

On the morning of August 19, 2000, I was in my office at 3 A.M., staring at the computer screen frustrated, with tears streaming down my cheeks, not knowing what to do. Then I did something radical, something I would not necessarily counsel anyone to do, but in my frustration I did it. Out loud I said to God, "God, I thought You called me to do fiction. I prayed and sought Your will. I thought you confirmed what You wanted me to do. Now I don't know what to do. God, if You want me to seriously pursue fiction, then please bring to me those words, 'When I run I feel your pleasure' one more time. If You don't, then I will put fiction out of my mind and simply pursue nonfiction because I know You're in that, too. Amen." After that prayer, I wiped my eyes and went to bed. But I was dead serious, and I was expecting God to answer my prayer.

The next morning when my eyes opened, the first thought that came to my mind was, "I wonder if God is going to bring me those words today? It would be truly supernatural if He did. What would be the odds? Then I would know for sure what to do."

My wife, Alanna, was already up and fixing breakfast in the kitchen. She knew nothing of my prayer earlier that morning, nor was she aware of my internal conflict. I had a stack of library books that needed to be returned, so I told Alanna I was going to run up to the library and drop them off, then we would eat breakfast. The library is only five minutes away. On the way to and from the library, I surfed all the channels on the car radio saying to myself, "Wouldn't it be neat if I happened across those words. I mean, what would be the odds?" I kept thinking of the incredible odds of my hearing those specific words from a twenty-year-old movie.

Then I did something different, and I'm so glad I did. I turned the radio off and out loud I said to God, "God, I don't want to create something that is not of You. If You want to bring me those words then You are going to have to do it completely separate from me. I don't want anything to do with it. If You don't bring them to me, then I'll just continue with nonfiction."

About the time I finished that prayer I was turning into our driveway. After Alanna and I finished eating and were cleaning up, the telephone rang and Alanna answered it. I was standing less than ten feet from her and the following is what I heard come out of my wife's mouth:

"Yes. That movie was *Chariots of Fire* and God spoke to Max through that movie when Eric Liddell said, 'When I run I feel God's pleasure.'"

As you can imagine, I about came unglued! Just a short time earlier I had told God that if He wanted to bring those words to me, He'd have to do it—and He did! But listen to how it happened and I think you'll get excited too. The person who called was my sister-in-law Lydia. She said she had been cleaning house that morning and the tune from the old movie about the Olympic runner who was a missionary to China just popped into her head. She said she hadn't thought of that movie for well over a decade, and something prompted her to call us to see if we knew its name! Lydia had not been to our church. She knew nothing of the sermon that touched me. Neither Alanna nor I had ever mentioned it to anyone in her family. As Lydia said, she had not thought of the movie for over a decade.

The other amazing thing is the fact that Alanna did not have to tell Lydia those words. She could have just said the name of the movie. And I must tell you something about my wife. She is a CPA and is one of the most ethical people I know. She is committed to justice. If ever I can count on someone to tell me the truth, it is Alanna. Of course, I was skeptical and was trying to figure out all the ways this could have happened by coincidence. "Maybe when Alanna told Lydia the name of the movie, I had a surprised look that prompted her to say those words?" Yet that doesn't account for the fact that Lydia called out of the clear blue about that particular movie. But Alanna told me that the whole time she was telling Lydia the words "when I run I feel God's pleasure" she was saying to herself, "This is bizarre. Why am I telling Lydia this?" Also, Alanna has supported me in my writing career, which hasn't always been easy. To follow God in this would mean an act of faith on Alanna's part as well as mine. If I had prompted her to say those words, believe me, she would have told me. She doesn't want me to miss God.

Think about it, because I sure have. I'm forty-three years old. That means I've had over 15,695 mornings in my life. Of those mornings only once has anyone ever called me out of the clear blue and asked for the name of that movie, or any movie for that matter. And Lydia just happened to call and ask about that movie on the only morning of my life that I had cried out to God to bring me those words if He wanted me to pursue what I was feeling in my heart. I would like to see a mathematician figure those odds.

Maybe I could call it a coincidence if it was a relatively new movie, but we're talking about a movie that is over twenty years old! And add to it the fact that Alanna just happened to spit out those words and didn't know why she was doing it. It would not have worked if I had answered the phone. It would have still been wild, but someone had to say those words. The Holy Spirit prompted Lydia to call and prompted Alanna. God set the whole thing up. He brought the words to me. I had no hand in it.

I don't understand why God would answer that prayer in such a dramatic way when so many more important prayers go seemingly unanswered. Yet I can't in good conscience dismiss this one as mere coincidence. God does indeed know where we live and is interested in the details of our lives.

As far as my fiction career goes, I'm working on my first novel, which I hope will be published soon.

The Dream That Wouldn't Go Away

Back when George Parker was a young livestock rancher north of Roosevelt, Utah, the news, one cold November morning, reported that a California doctor and his wife were missing on a flight from Custer, South Dakota, to Salt Lake City. As a student pilot, George had just completed his first cross-country flight with an instructor, though he had only twenty solo hours.

Paying close attention to all radio reports on the search, George was very disturbed two days later by a newscast saying that Dr. Robert Dykes and his wife, Margery, both in their late twenties and parents of two young children, were not likely to be found until spring—and maybe not even then. They had been missing four days, and the temperature had been below zero every night. There seemed little chance for their survival without food and proper clothing.

That night before he retired, George prayed to God for these two people he didn't know. "Dear God, if they're still alive, send someone to them so they will be able to get back to their family."

After a while he drifted off to sleep. In a dream George saw a red plane on a snow-swept ridge and two people waving for help. He awoke with a start. *Was it the Dykeses? What color is their plane?* He didn't remember any of the news reports ever mentioning it.

He couldn't get back to sleep for some time and kept reasoning that because he had been thinking of the couple before falling asleep, it was natural for him to dream of them. But when he finally did go to sleep, the dream came again! A red plane on a ridge—but now farther away. George still saw two people waving and could now see snow-covered mountain peaks in the background.

He got out of bed and spread out the only air chart he owned. It covered a remote area in Utah—the High Uintas region, along the Wyoming-Utah border. The Dykeses' flight plan presumably had to pass over this range. George was familiar with the rugged terrain because he had fished and hunted it as a boy. It was a huge area about the size of the state of Connecticut. Finding a small plane in those rugged mountains would be like looking for a needle in a haystack.

His eyes scanned the names on the chart—Burro Peak, Painters Basin, Kings Peak, Gilbert Peak.

Again George went to bed. And again, incredibly, the dream returned! Now the plane was barely in sight. He could see the valley below. Then it came to him in a flash—Painters Basin and Gilbert Peak! George rose in a cold sweat. It was daylight.

Turning on the news, he found there had been no sign of the plane, and the search had been called off. All that day, doing chores around the ranch, he could think of nothing but the Dykeses and the dream. He felt God had shown him where those people were and that they were alive. But who would believe him, and what could he do about it? George knew he wasn't qualified to search for them himself. He knew, too, that even trying to explain his dream to his flight instructor, a stern taskmaster named Joe Mower, would have him laughed out of the hanger.

George decided to go to the small rural airport anyway. When he arrived, a teenage boy who was watching the place told him Joe had gone to town for the mail.

The presence that had been nudging him all morning seemed to say, "Go!" George had the boy help him push an Aeronca plane out. When he asked George where he was going, George said, "To look for the Dykeses." He gave the plane a throttle and was on his way.

Trimming out, he began a steady climb and headed for Uinta Canyon. He knew what he was doing was unwise, even dangerous, but the danger seemed a small thing compared to what he felt in his heart.

As George turned east near Painters Basin, he was beginning to lose faith in his dream; there was no sign of the missing plane. The high winds, downdrafts, and rough air were giving him trouble in the small sixty-five-horsepower plane. Terribly disappointed as well as frightened, George was about to turn back when suddenly there it was! A red plane on Gilbert Peak, just as he had seen in his dream.

Coming closer, he could see two people waving. George was so happy he began to cry. "Thank you, God," he said over and over. Opening the plane's window, he waved at the Dykeses and wigwagged his wings to let them know he saw them. Then George said a prayer to God to help him get back to the airport safely.

Thirty minutes later George was on the ground, and when he taxied up and cut the motor, an angry Joe Mower was there to greet him.

"You're grounded," Joe hollered. "You had no permission to take that plane up."

"Joe," George said quickly, "I know I did wrong, but listen. I found the Dykeses and they need help."

"You're crazy," Joe said, and he continued to yell. George's finding that plane in an hour and a half when hundreds of planes had searched in vain for nearly a week was more than Joe could believe.

Finally George turned away from Joe, went straight for a telephone, and called the CAP (Civil Air Patrol) in Salt Lake City. When they answered, he asked if there had been any word on the Dykeses' plane. They said there was no chance of their being alive now and that the search had ended.

"Well, I've found them," George said, "and they're both alive."

Behind him, Joe stopped chewing him out, his eyes wide, and his mouth open.

"I'll round up food and supplies," George continued to the CAP, "and the people here will get them out as soon as possible." The CAP gave George the go-ahead.

Everyone at the airport went into action. Within one hour they were on their way. A local expert pilot, Hal Crumbo, would fly in the supplies. George would lead the way in another plane. He wasn't grounded for long.

Back in the air, they headed for the high peaks. Hal's plane was bigger and faster than the Aeronca George was in. Hal was flying out ahead and above him. When they got to Painters Basin, at 11,000 feet, they met the severe downdrafts again. George could see Hal circling above him and knew he was in sight of the downed plane and ready to drop supplies. Since George couldn't go any higher, he turned around.

Back at the airport he joined a three-man ground rescue party that would attempt to reach the couple by horseback.

Another rescue party had already left from the Wyoming side of the mountains. For the next twenty-four hours the ground party hiked through fierce winds and six-foot snowdrifts. At 12,000 feet, on a ridge near Gilbert Peak, they stopped. In the distance, someone was yelling. Urging their frozen feet forward, they pressed on, tremendously excited. Suddenly, about a hundred yards in front of them was the fuselage of a small red plane rammed into a snowbank. Nearby, two people waved their arms wildly.

Charging ahead, they shouted with joy. At about the same time the ground party reached the Dykeses, the other rescue party was coming over the opposite ridge.

After much hugging and thanking, George learned what a miracle the Dykeses' survival was. They had had nothing to eat but a candy bar, and their clothing was scant—Mrs. Dykes had a fur coat, but her husband had only a topcoat. The altitude made starting a fire impossible, and at night they huddled together in their downed plane, too afraid to go asleep.

"We had all but given up, had even written notes as to who should look after the children," Mrs. Dykes said. Then, turning to George, she said, "But when we saw your plane, it was the most wonderful thing... our prayers answered, a dream come true."

"Yes," George said, smiling, suddenly feeling as Solomon in the Bible must have felt after he received a visit from the Lord one night in a dream (see 1 Kings 3:5–14).

George's dream, like Solomon's, had occurred for a reason. In His own special way, God gave him that dream in order to help give life to two others. Even in the most mysterious of ways, God had shown George He is always there, always listening. He had heard George's prayers and the Dykeses' prayers and had answered in His own infallible way.[15]

Yes, God still answers prayer. When we are living in desperate dependence upon Him instead of living in our comfort zone, we give God an opportunity to do the miraculous. And as with the apostle Paul, sometimes God will not remove the thorn and give us His sufficient grace, but sometimes He will, by His supernatural means, pluck that thorn out. Either way, God is faithful.

> "Believe me when I say that I am in the Father and
> the Father is in me; or at least believe on the
> evidence of the miracles themselves."
> —*Jesus (John 14:11)*

CHAPTER TWELVE

AN INTERVIEW
WITH A FORMER
ATHEIST

*T*he following statement appeared in my hometown newspaper's opinion section some time back. Take a look (emphasis added):

Many People Don't Trust in God

I strongly object to posting the statement "In God We Trust" on the walls of public schools or any other government building. I don't like the fact that we have it on our money or that we refer to God in the Pledge of Allegiance. Prayers in the legislature should be silent, and there should be no Bibles in our court-rooms.

Like many taxpayers and citizens of this country, *I do not trust in God. In fact, many have come to accept the fact that there is no such thing as God. God is a myth—a fairy tale, a kind of Santa Claus figure; comforting to children and useful in controlling the gullible masses. We might just as well post "I believe in the tooth fairy" on our walls.*

Many Christians seem to have a burning need to spread their brand of dogma. It is not enough that they brainwash their own children with biblical fantasy; they seem compelled to "save" my children as well. Thanks, but no thanks.

I have tried to guide my children in their journey toward becoming responsible, *ethical adults by emphasizing facts, not fiction; provable science, not faith-based malarkey.* We place our trust very carefully upon ourselves, our family, and good friends. We trust our public officials to a point; we trust our police department. I trust my dog. This trust was earned by virtue of repeated, reliable, observable behavior.

I am truly astounded by those who continue to trust in God.

At one time I would have been intimidated by the above comments. I can remember being singled out by a professor while at the University of Mississippi and ridiculed for my faith. I had no idea how to respond to his accusations. But now, after my twenty-year quest, I not only feel confident, but I am certain that the most brilliant minds in society are with me.

The above writer stated that he believed in "emphasizing facts, not fiction; provable science, not faith-based malarkey," that he was "truly astounded by those who continue to trust in God." Unfortunately, the humanistic society in which we live has fed us so much of this type of thinking that masses of Christians and non-Christians alike feel that in order to believe in an all-powerful God one must throw away reason and accept everything by blind faith. Nothing could be further from the truth. Not only is it reasonable to believe in an all-powerful God, it is good science. The problem with people like the above gentleman is that they don't examine the facts. If they did, they would no longer be atheists. To refuse to believe in God, one must make a concerted effort to ignore the plain facts.

Psalm 53:1 says, "The fool says in his heart, 'There is no God.'" Romans 1:20 adds, "For since the creation of the world God's invisible qualities—his eternal power and divine nature—have been clearly seen, being understood from what has been made, so that men are without excuse."

My goal in this chapter is not to present all of the evidences and arguments for the existence of God and the resurrection of Jesus. That would take another book. I merely wish to refute the claim that belief in God is simplistic and not good science by letting you hear what some of the most brilliant minds in the world, both past and contemporary, have to say about the subject. Please read their credentials. These are not preachers or evangelists; they are top scientists and philosophers. Then I wish to show how all of this relates to desperate dependence.

Brilliant Minds of Old

"The scientist's religious feeling takes the form of a rapturous amazement at the harmony of natural law, *which reveals an intelligence of such superiority* that, compared with it, all the systematic thinking and acting of human beings is an utterly insignificant reflection.... I defend the Good God against the idea of a continuous game of dice."[16]

—Albert Einstein (emphasis added)

"The supreme God exists necessarily, and by the same necessity He exists always and everywhere.... He endureth forever, and is everywhere present; and by existing always and everywhere, He constitutes duration and space.... In Him are all things contained and moved."[17]

—Sir Isaac Newton

"The ardors of piety agree—that nothing is of us or of our works—that all is of God."[18]

—Ralph Waldo Emerson

"Here is my creed. I believe in one God, Creator of the Universe. That He governs it by His providence. That He ought to be worshiped."[19]

—Benjamin Franklin

"In the name of God, I William Shakespeare... God be praised, do make and ordain this, my last will and testament in manner and form following. That is to say, first I commend my soul into the hands of God my Creator, hoping and assuredly believing, through the only merits of Jesus Christ, my saviour, to be made partaker of eternal life, and my body to the earth whereof it is made."[20]

—William Shakespeare

"God's mercy is over all his works."[21]

—Jonathan Swift

"Each will have to make his own choice: to oppose the will of God, building upon the sands the unstable house of his brief illusive life, or to join in the eternal, deathless movement of true life in accordance with God's will."[22]

—Leo Tolstoy

"The proof of an intelligent God as the author of creation stood as infinity to one against any other hypothesis for ultimate causation."[23]

—astronomer Pierre-Simon Laplace

"All nature cries to us that He exists, that there is a Supreme Intelligence, a power immense, an order admirable, and all teaches us our dependence."[24]

—Voltaire

"Everything in the world shows either the unhappy condition of man, or the mercy of God; either the weakness of man without God, or the power of man assisted by God."[25]

—Blaise Pascal

"Cathedrals are beautiful and rise high into the blue sky, but the nests of the swallows are the building of God."[26]

—Victor Hugo

Brilliant Contemporary Minds

"It is not difficult for me to have this faith, for it is incontrovertible that where there is a plan there is intelligence—an orderly, unfolding universe testifies to the truth of the most majestic statement ever uttered—'In the beginning, God.'"[27]

—Arthur H. Compton

Arthur Compton won the Nobel prize for physics in 1927 and taught physics at the University of Chicago.

"So many essential conditions are necessary for life to exist on our earth that it is mathematically impossible that all of them could exist in proper relationship by chance on any one earth at one time."[28]

—A. Cressy Morrison

A. Cressy Morrison is the past president of the New York Academy of Sciences.

"Today as we ponder the unique architecture of the molecular systems that make up life, I am sure that I will not be the last person to conclude that 'there must be an architect.' I cannot possibly conceive how such a system could ever evolve."[29]

—Bob Hosken

Bob Hosken, who holds a doctorate in biochemistry, is senior lecturer in food technology at the University of Newcastle, Australia. He has published more than fifty research papers in the areas of protein structure and function, food technology, and food product development.

"God has allowed us the privilege of living in a time when great mysteries are being uncovered. No previous era knew about quantum mechanics, relativity, subatomic particles, supernovas, ageless photons, or DNA. They all reveal the stunning genius of a God who spoke a time-space-matter-light universe into existence, balanced it with impossible requirements of precision, and then gifted it with life."[30]

—Richard A. Swenson

Richard Swenson, M.D., is a physician and a futurist. He taught at the University of Wisconsin Medical School for fifteen years.

"Aside from the brain, biological cells are probably the most complicated entities on the face of the earth, and possibly, hubris notwithstanding, the most complicated entities in the universe, far more complicated than we would imagine from an external view of the organisms they combine to make. The complexity of life's biology is held within its internal processes, but dressed in the simplicity of our outer bodies. Anyone who thinks nature is simple should take a short user-friendly course in how just one cell 'evolves' into two cells, and then marvel at the vast amount of information required to bring about this single step and then wonder at its source.... The hidden face of God is found in the details."[31]

—Gerald Schroeder

Gerald Schroeder earned a doctorate at the Massachusetts Institute of Technology before moving to laboratories at Weizmann Institute, the Hebrew University, and the Volcani Research Institute in Israel. His work has been reported in *Time, Newsweek,* and *Scientific American.*

"The odds against a universe like ours coming out of something like a Big Bang are enormous. I think there are clearly religious implications."[32]

—Stephen Hawking, British physicist

"As a scientist, I look at the world around me, and observe engineering mechanisms of such remarkable complexity that I am drawn to the conclusion of intelligent design being behind such complex order.... No scientist is entirely objective. We are always governed by our assumptions. If a scientist does not believe in God, then his starting point of atheism will be bound to affect his judgment as he looks at the world around him. If his mind is closed to the possibility of a designer, his own assumption will force him to adopt what to many will seem an 'unlikely' explanation for what he observes."[33]

—Andrew McIntosh

Andrew McIntosh holds doctorates in the theory of combustion from the Cranfield Institute of Technology and mathematics from the University of Wales.

"When archaeologists come across a smooth, cylindrical clay structure with walls consistently about the same thickness, a flat bottom that allows the structure to stand upright, and an opening in the top, it is a sure sign to them that some type of intelligent civilization was responsible for producing that clay pot. It is such a simple deduction to make—it is obvious that an ordered structure such as a clay pot could not have come about by chance. One can see that even the smallest amount of order exhibited in a simple clay pot is almost completely beyond the reach of random processes. That is why archaeologists know that a clay pot is a clear signature of civilization; orderliness is evidence of design.... Step back now and consider: how is this different from the formation of life from non-living chemicals? To be sure, there is a difference; the generation of a living organism from simple non-living chemicals is infinitely less likely to occur. Living organisms are so much more complex than is a clay pot that an adequate comparison cannot even be made. What person would want to believe that a clay pot arose by chance processes? The orderliness of living things and their mind-boggling complexity are surely unmistakable indications that this creation did not come about by random and disorderly chance processes."[34]

—John P. Marcus

John Marcus holds a doctorate in biological chemistry from the University of Michigan.

"I accept the Creator God of Scripture, partly because scientific data seems to require a supernatural element—an intelligent designer. According to a *Newsweek* cover story entitled 'Science Finds God,' well-respected scientists are finding that data from nature are commensurate with belief in God. The astronomer Allen Sandage says, 'It was my science that drove me to the conclusion that the world is much more complicated than can be explained by science. It is only through the supernatural that I can understand the mystery of existence.' As I develop my understanding of origins, it includes reason based on evidence from both nature and Scripture."[35]

—Ben Clausen

Ben Clausen is a research scientist at the Geoscience Research Institute, Loma Linda, California. He holds a doctorate in nuclear physics from the University of Colorado. He has been a research associate in the physics department at the University of Virginia.

Shall I go on? I could quote from literally hundreds of top scientists and thinkers. The fact is, some of the most brilliant minds in the world believe that God is good science. And the more technology uncovers, the more of God we see. Though some would label me simple-minded and though there are certainly aspects of the God's workings that I don't understand and I've felt my share of pain in life, I cannot in good conscience deny all that I've seen over the years—the answers to prayer and all the evidence in nature. God has come through for me too many times. If I am labeled simple-minded, so be it. I'm in good company!

A Hunger for Truth

Eric Dimari is one of the most intelligent men you will meet. He is a favorite teacher at one of the local public schools in my area. Eric was raised in New York City by hardcore atheist parents and was himself an atheist. Yet he broke ranks with the atheists and now is a committed Christ follower even though he has had his share of pain. You see, Eric is the father of an autistic child. When I spoke with Eric I wanted to know how he came to such strong faith in God, despite all the unanswered questions, the pain, and being raised atheist.

"Growing up, I naturally adopted my parents' beliefs," Eric said. "Their argument against God made sense to me. 'How could there be a good God with all the evil in the world?' And that's the attitude I picked up."

All through high school and college if people said they were Christian, Eric had a good time sparring with them. He would throw at them the same questions his parents used. In addition to the pain and suffering argument, he would ask them, "How can you say Christianity is true? What about Islam? What about the Indian gods? What about Buddhism? Are you saying that they are all wrong?" Eric enjoyed arguing. It was fun trying to convince someone that his faith was foolish.

While he was in his sophomore year of college, Eric began to develop a hunger for truth. He sensed something out there was called truth. He had no idea what it was. It still had nothing to do with God at the time. But he wanted to know what truth was. Eric spent some time considering it and came to the conclusion that "goodness" was truth. If you were a good person then you were living in the truth.

That lasted for a while, then it evolved into something more. He sensed that there was something deeper than "goodness." Then he came to the conclusion that "love" was truth. So he said he wanted to try to love people. Mind you, everything was still very atheistic. God was still not even a consideration in all of this. At the time, Eric had no idea that it was God who was drawing him to Himself. So he went a while believing that "love" was truth. Yet he still hungered to make sure that he was living in truth and he still sensed deeply that he was missing something.

At this time, Eric had a friend whose girlfriend was a Christian. She asked him, "Eric, do you believe in God?"

Eric responded, "No. But I'll think about it." That was the extent of their conversation. After that he didn't see her again. But the question sparked a desire in Eric to know if there really was a God. If that was the truth, then he wanted to know.

He was going to college in upstate New York in a quaint little town and would take long walks. While walking he would ponder these questions. One night, he said, "God, if You are there, I want to know." If He wasn't there, that was okay by Eric. His life was fine. This was not a crisis. In fact, it was probably one of the happiest times of his life. Nevertheless, Eric said, "God, if You are there, show me."

On another night he had gone to a party and met his roommate from the previous year. Eric had really looked forward to seeing him, but his former roommate was as cold as ice to him and Eric couldn't understand it because he had been a good friend. The way he treated him really hurt, and Eric walked home that night, dejected, saying to himself, "There is no God. It is true. There is just too much evil and sadness in the world for God to be real. That's it, my search is over."

But then something rose up inside of him and he cried out, "God, if You are really there, then show me now!" Instantly and surprisingly, there was an unexpected tingling in Eric's head, and it felt as if his brain were going to explode into a hundred pieces. Then, out of his gut—that's the only way he could describe it—came the words J-E-S-U-S! G-O-D! At that moment, God revealed Himself to Eric. Eric says, "I had no bias or preconceived notions. If it had been Buddha or Allah, it would have been fine with me. Jesus as God was a complete surprise. I had no previous knowledge that the Bible referred to Jesus as God. My Bible knowledge was nil."

From that point on Eric knew that Jesus was real—there was no doubt about it. Since then he has never doubted the existence of God. That's not to say he hasn't had issues. Eric is like me. He's still very much a skeptic.

Eric honestly believes that hardcore atheists and agnostics stay there because they do not want to know truth. "To say that the universe with all its complexities and interworkings all happened by chance is just ridiculous. To me it is intellectually unsound not to believe that there is a designer behind creation," Eric said. "Maybe I'm wrong on this point, but ultimately I believe you must have a personal encounter with God to truly believe."

Naturally, having a son with autism has been a trial for him. "Knowing God," he says, "doesn't take away the pain. When you become a Christian your perspective changes and you realize that this life is a very small part of our existence. And if this small part of my existence is difficult, I have a wonderful eternity coming."

One of Eric's favorite Scriptures is Romans 8:18: "I consider that our present sufferings are not worth comparing with the glory that will be revealed in us." (Where have we heard that before?) It brings great comfort to his heart knowing that his son Michael is going to spend eternity with Jesus. No matter how much pain and suffering he experiences here on earth, he's going to spend eternity with God.

"I don't know if you would understand this if you don't have a mentally handicapped child," said Eric, "but I sometimes think, *What is the worst case scenario? What happens if after I die, Michael ends up as one of these destitute people on the street?* Of course, that strikes horror in me—terror sometimes. But then I say, 'worst case scenario,' which I really don't think will happen, 'and after that he's going to spend eternity with Jesus and that pain will be all taken away.'"

Eric does not doubt the goodness of God when he wonders why this happened to his son. He simply knows that in this life, difficult things happen. Some days he loses his perspective and, like the rest of us, is dominated by worry and fear, but that's not what has dominated his life.

My friend, the God of the universe is alive. He created your brain with its capacity to hold the equivalent of twenty-five million books—one thousand times that of a Cray-2 supercomputer. Your brain is the most complex and orderly arrangement of matter in the universe. He designed your eyes, which take pictures and develop them instantly! He programmed your individual DNA with over a thousand encyclopedias' worth of information in just one cell.

He also encoded into the spider the ability to spin a perfect web and into each seed the information it needs to grow into a specific plant. This God who keeps the universe going cares for you and knows right where you are. He's calling you to trust Him with desperate dependence.

> "I praise you because I am fearfully
> and wonderfully made;
> your works are wonderful, I know that full well."
> —David (Ps. 139:14)

CHAPTER THIRTEEN

GOD'S BRUTAL HONESTY

"Jesus knows how you feel."
—*Max Lucado*

rust me, it is much easier to write about success and happiness than pain, failure, and weakness. Now don't get me wrong—there is a place for success and happiness. God wants that for us. But the reality is that we are weak, life is hard, and sometimes it just doesn't make sense.

On September 11, many good people, some with children and spouses and dreams, woke up and got dressed for their jobs at the World Trade Center. Perhaps they watched the morning news as they ate their bagel or grabbed a breakfast bar and then hurried out the door. Some frantically pulled their kids together just in time to catch the school bus. But none had a clue that later that day they would be jumping out a window to their deaths below. You saw the pictures. It's tough. We don't like to see them. Yet they are reality. It happened.

My friend John was a motorcycle enthusiast. He owned a Harley-Davidson and loved his freedom. That all changed in a matter of seconds when he dove into a river, severing his spinal cord. Today he is a quadriplegic living in a nursing home. What John wants to know now is, "How do I go on? Where can I find hope? Is there a reason in all this pain?"

In all fairness to atheists and agnostics, their argument does have some credibility: "If God is so good, then why does He seem so absent?"

Charles Templeton, one of the world's most popular agnostics, said what finally convinced him to be agnostic was the fact that God didn't send rain. *Life* magazine was doing a story on a devastating drought in northern Africa and on the cover was a picture of a woman holding her dead child.

Templeton said, "She was holding her dead baby in her arms and looking up to heaven with the most forlorn expression. I looked at it and thought, 'Is it possible to believe that there is a loving or caring Creator when all this woman needed was rain?' How could a loving God do this to that woman? Who runs the rain? I don't; you don't. He does—or that's what I thought. But when I saw that photograph, I immediately knew it is not possible for this to happen and for there to be a loving God. There was no way. Who else but a fiend could destroy a baby and virtually kill its mother with agony—when all that was needed was rain?"[36]

Why didn't God send rain? Why did three thousand innocent people die on September 11? Why is my son deaf? After twelve chapters, we are right back to the same old question of *why?*

So far, we have heard from many people whose faith was actually strengthened through their pain and who testify to God's faithfulness. We've seen stories of God's miraculous answers to prayer. We've learned about storms and thorns and building strong foundations. In the previous chapter we saw that despite the injustices in the world, great minds concur that the evidence is strong in favor of an intelligent designer. We even heard from a former atheist who had a dramatic conversion. All of this is helpful, but it comes just a bit short of giving me the full comfort and courage I need to move successfully through this life.

God's Provision

Do you know what true success is? The definition is critical to this chapter and book. True success has very little to do with money, possessions, or any of the other symbols by which society today gauges success. True biblical success is coming to that place in life where you want what you have and you have what you want. You're content. You're at peace. When you look at your house or your car, it may not be exactly what you dreamed of, but that's okay because it's God's provision. You start to see everything as God's provision—your spouse, your job, your extended family.

The important things in your life are the people God has surrounded you with and getting to know Christ more intimately. It's where you can say, along with Paul, "I know what it is to be in need, and I know what it is to have plenty. I have learned the secret of being content in any and every situation, whether well fed or hungry, whether living in plenty or in want. I can do everything through him who gives me strength" (Phil. 4:12–13).

It's a place where the closer you get to God the more aware you are of your own sinfulness, and you recognize your daily dependence on Him. It's a place where you have learned never to pray, "God, give me what I deserve," because you know that the moment God gives you what you deserve the ground will split open and you will plummet straight to hell.

My friend, true success comes when we are living moment by moment in desperate dependence on God. When you live there, even walking to the mailbox becomes an adventure because you are alive to His presence. Personal holiness becomes personal whole-i-ness. You begin to understand that God hates the things He hates because they cause pain and keep you from being the whole person He desires you to be.

It's a place of quiet confidence and rest in the Lord where we experience God's best in life's toughest situations. That is true success, and the only way it comes is through trials and tribulation—through the refiner's fire. And that is one reason why God allows pain and suffering. He didn't cause it, but He will use it for our good.

Life Is Hard

Out of everything brought forth thus far, the next point is perhaps the one that gives me the most comfort. It's what helps me come to terms with the unanswerable "whys" in life. What is it? It is the fact of God's brutal honesty.

The Word of God never denies that life is hard. In fact, the Bible pulls no punches and doesn't whitewash a thing. It tells it exactly as it is—that sometimes the innocent suffer. In reality, the very first family was about as dysfunctional as you can get. Early on, evil got the upper hand when Cain murdered his brother Abel, who was doing right. The good guy got the ax, and people have been killing each other ever since.

God doesn't deny a thing. He said that evil entered the world when sin entered the world—that humanity is fallen and is under the curse, that Satan is now the god of this world. History, both biblical and secular, bears this out. Though humans do have some good in them, they also have an incredible bent toward evil. If you don't think so, just look around—murders, rapes, wars, children being abducted and abused, suicide bombers, and pornography are common. I think you get the picture. We live in a nasty world. And though technology has made incredible advances, Homo sapiens as a species is *not* getting any better. Yet out of love for His creation, God chose to turn it around—to work all this evil out for the good. He uses the evil and suffering in the world as an anvil to mold a people who will reflect His character.

His brutal honesty never once denies that injustice occurs and bad things happen to good people. From Genesis to Revelation, the Bible is chock-full of examples.

Abel did the right thing and was murdered (see Genesis 4).

Joseph did the right thing by not sleeping with his master's wife and was falsely accused and thrown into prison (see Genesis 37–41).

Elijah the prophet did mighty miracles and was taken up to heaven in a whirlwind (see 2 Kings 2:11). Elisha did twice as many miracles, but suffered and died from a terminal illness (see 2 Kings 13:14).

Uriah was a faithful soldier. He went to battle to fight for his beloved King David, and while he was gone, the king slept with his wife and then had him murdered (see 2 Samuel 11–12).

Job was innocent and he suffered through robbers who stole his wealth, wildfires that burned his fields, and a tornado that killed his children. Then he broke out in boils (see Job 1–2).

Yes, the Bible is brutally honest. It even addresses unfortunate accidents. In Luke 13:4 Jesus mentions eighteen men who died when a tower collapsed and declared that they were just innocent victims. God never tries to pull the wool over our eyes. He doesn't try to cover for the fact that bad stuff happens. And the fact that the Bible doesn't try to convince me otherwise gives me great comfort.

The Bible's brutal honesty is strong evidence of the validity of the Christian faith. Why? Because humans could have never thought it up. Former atheist C. S. Lewis explained it eloquently in *Mere Christianity:*

Reality, in fact, is usually something you could not have guessed. That is one of the reasons I believe

Christianity. It is a religion you could not have guessed. If it offered us just the kind of universe we had always expected, I should feel we were making it up. But, in fact, it is not the sort of thing anyone would have made up. It has just that queer twist about it that real things have.... What is the problem? A universe that contains much that is obviously bad and apparently meaningless, but containing creatures like ourselves who know that it is bad and meaningless.[37]

But then God did something amazing and radical. He didn't just point out our dilemma as a species, but He did something about it. God became one of us and entered into our sufferings. In all other religions, man has to jump through a thousand hoops to get to God, but in Christianity God came down to us.

He did this so we could understand Him more and He could understand us more. I'm reminded of a story I heard one time of a man who was working in his workshop one cold winter day. As he looked out over his snowy backyard, he noticed a little bird freezing to death. The man went out in the snow and tried and tried to coax the bird into the warm workshop. But the frightened bird struggled and resisted. The man thought, "If only I could become a bird, then I could fly to it and show it the way." As soon as he had that thought, the man fell on his knees because he realized that God had done that very same thing when He came into the world as Jesus.

Yes, my friend, God feels your pain. He knows what it is

like to suffer. He experienced His own suffering. Jesus wept at the news of His friend Lazarus' death. He certainly knew injustice and betrayal. His own disciples abandoned Him in His darkest hour. In the garden, Jesus begged the Father to somehow let Him forgo the Cross. But the Father said no.

And when Jesus died on the cross He experienced suffering and pain, both physical and emotional, to its absolute fullest. The good news is that all that suffering was nailed to the cross with Him, and when He rose from the grave, He left it there. Because of His resurrection, He has sent the Holy Spirit, God's Spirit, to be a very relevant Comforter to us. That's why Jeremiah could write, "O LORD, my strength and my fortress, my refuge in time of distress" (Jer. 16:19). We can run to God in times of distress because He knows how we feel.

My friend John, though now a quadriplegic, can move on. He can live in hope and abundance, because God's Spirit feels his pain and is there to comfort and strengthen him. It's true. When the wind and the waves are thrashing around, when we can't see what lies ahead, when it appears our boat is going under, hold on. Have courage. Jesus is there. Cling to Him in desperate dependence and soon the storm will pass, the sea will calm, and you *will* make it safely to the other shore.

"Immediately Jesus reached out his
hand and caught him."
—*Matt. 14:31*

Your Life Journey

Desperate Dependence

A guide for personal reflection

or group discussion

Chapter 1: Desperate Dependence

1. Do you think God wants us to come to the end of ourselves before we can experience His best? Why?

2. Have you ever hit rock bottom and cried out to God to provide?

3. What does the "safe zone" mean to you?

4. How could God become your source in life?

5. Is it realistic to "be of good cheer" when we feel pain?

6. Discuss Johnny Nicosia's statement: "I know that God loved me too much to leave me as I was."

7. At the end of this chapter, are you encouraged or discouraged? Why?

Chapter 2: Recognizing Christ in the Storm

1. Have you ever obeyed what you thought God was saying and ended up in a storm? Did you experience Jesus there?

2. Why did Jesus tell the disciples to go to the other side of the lake?

3. Why did the disciples not recognize Jesus when He came to them on the water?

4. Why did Peter get out of the boat and walk to Jesus?

5. Have you ever felt the silence of God that C. S. Lewis described?

Chapter 3: A Faith That Pleases

1. Explain the two aspects of faith discussed in this chapter.

2. Do you know anyone who has gone through something difficult yet still has strong faith? What did you learn from him or her?

3. Why does God deliver some from difficulty and not others?

4. Why did Jesus leave John the Baptist in prison?

5. Have you found yourself in a situation where you must trust God even though you don't understand what is going on?

Chapter 4: Practical Insights from Job

1. Why did God let Satan attack Job?

2. Have you ever had friends like Job's friends? Have you ever been like Job's comforters?

3. Why did God rebuke Job's comforters and not Job?

4. Was Job wrong for questioning God?

5. If God said Job had not sinned, then why did Job repent in dust and ashes?

6. How has this chapter helped you become a better friend and comforter?

Chapter 5: Conduits of Comfort

1. What is the difference between a victim mentality and being a conduit of God's comfort?

2. Discuss the statement "The great need in the world today is not for more gifted people, but for more broken people."

3. What are some positive characteristics of broken people?

4. How can God turn a valley of pain into a spring of refreshment?

5. Have you ever been disappointed by God? If so, did the experience hinder you from moving forward?

6. Do you know someone who is a good example of the statement "comforted to comfort"? Describe his or her life.

Chapter 6: Living on Purpose

1. Do you believe you know God's will for your life? If so, why? If not, why not?

2. Has God called you to a specific task?

3. Do you have a deep desire to do something you think God may be leading you to?

4. Are you afraid that if you desire something then it's probably not from God?

5. If we love God, does He work through our desires?

6. What is God's ultimate purpose for us?

7. Why does God want a people conformed to Christ's image?

Chapter 7: When Past Failures Haunt

1. How can the young man who killed his best friend in an auto accident move forward in life? Could you forgive him? Could you forgive yourself if you were in that situation?

2. What does Isaiah 1:18 mean when it says that no matter how deep the stain of your sins, God can remove it?

3. Explain and discuss your view of God's sovereignty. If God is sovereign do we really still have free will?

4. How does the fact that we can't live the Christian life in our own power relate to the story of David and Mephibosheth?

5. What does Paul mean when he says, "Forgetting what is behind and straining toward what is ahead"? Can we really forget our past failures?

Chapter 8: Earthquake Praise

1. Do you sometimes find it hard to praise God?

2. Do you ever get bogged down in bad news?

3. Why do you think God responds to our praise?

4. Have you ever praised God in a difficult situation? What was the result?

5. What does it mean to grieve, but not as those with no hope?

Chapter 9: What's in the Well

1. Discuss the statement "Crises don't make you who you are, they reveal who you are."

2. What are some ways you can trust God during "normal" times?

3. What did God mean when He told Paul in 2 Corinthians 12:9 (NKJV), "My grace is sufficient for you, for My strength is made perfect in weakness"?

4. Are you consistent in the basics? Explain.

5. Can you relate to God as "Abba"?

6. Has the body of Christ ever been there for you during a tough time? Has the body of Christ ever let you down?

7. Do you have a strong house? If so, why? If not, what changes do you need to make?

Chapter 10: Thorns of Grace

1. What is meant by the statement "He who is used greatly must suffer deeply"?

2. Do you find that when adversity surfaces in your life you depend on God more? If so, why?

3. Do you tend to not call on God as much when times are good?

4. Do you look forward to being with the Lord?

5. Why do you think God didn't remove Paul's thorn in the flesh? What are some thorns in your flesh?

6. How can God's allowing thorns to stay help us become more Christlike?

Chapter 11: God Still Does Miracles

1. Do you believe God does miracles today?

2. Give some examples of answered prayer in your own life.

3. How does hearing stories of miracles affect your faith?

4. Are you a skeptic? If so, why?

5. Have you ever believed God for something important that didn't happen? What encouraged you to keep your faith?

6. In several of the stories, the people felt an inner prompting in their spirits to move in a direction and then they acted on it. Have you ever felt God prompting you?

7. How can you judge whether an inner prompting is from the Holy Spirit or your own flesh?

Chapter 12: An Interview with a Former Atheist

1. What is the difference between an atheist and an agnostic?

2. Why do you believe some people are so anti-God?

3. Have you ever thought that faith and science aren't compatible?

4. Consider some of the amazing wonders of nature, such as a spider spinning a web, or the human brain or eye, then discuss them.

5. John Marcus pointed out that when archeologists find

something such as a piece of pottery they assume it was created by an intelligent source. Yet when scientists see something much more sophisticated, such as the brain or eye, they refuse to acknowledge a creator. What do you think about order coming from disorder?

Chapter 13: God's Brutal Honesty

1. What do you think about the atheist's and agnostic's argument that God must not exist or be good or omnipotent because evil infuses the world?

2. Does the author's definition of true success scare you or appeal to you?

3. Can you see how God uses pain and suffering to refine us?

4. How do you feel about the Bible's brutal honesty? Does it comfort you?

5. Do you think the world is getting better or worse?

6. Does God's becoming flesh and blood like us bring you comfort?

Notes

1. C. S. Lewis, *Mere Christianity* (New York: Simon & Schuster, 1980), 94.

2. C. S. Lewis, *A Grief Observed* (New York: Bantam, 1961), 4.

3. Norman Williams, *Terror at Tenerife* (Van Nuys, Calif.: Bible Voice, 1977), 63–67.

4. F. F. Bruce, *The Epistle to the Hebrews* (Grand Rapids, Mich.: Eerdmans, 1990), 328–330.

5. Roy Hicks, *A Small Book About God* (Sisters, Ore.: Multnomah, 1997), 161.

6. Philip Yancey, *Disappointment with God* (Grand Rapids, Mich.: Zondervan, 1988), 181.

7. Henry Blackaby, *Hearing God's Voice* (Nashville: Broadman & Holman, 2002), 146.

8. Marjorie Holmes, *How Can I Find You, God?* (New York: Doubleday, 1975), 98.

9. Gregory A. Boyd, *Letters from a Skeptic* (Colorado Springs: Cook, 1994), 9, postscript.

10. Merlin Carothers, *Praise Works!* (Escondido, Calif.: Carothers, 1973), 1–3.

11. John Claypool, *Tracks of a Fellow Struggler* (Waco, Tex.: Word, 1974), 82–83.

12. Merlin Carothers, *Praise News*, March 2003, 1.

13. John Wimber, *Power Evangelism* (San Francisco: Harper & Row, 1986), 32–34.

14. John Van Diest, *Unsolved Miracles* (Sisters, Ore.: Multnomah, 1997), 187–191.

15. George Hunt, *The Best Stories from Guideposts* (Wheaton, Ill.: Tyndale House, 1987), 95–98.

16. Pierre Speziali, ed., *Albert Einstein–Michele Basso Correspondence, 1903–1955* (Paris: Hermann, 1972), 425.

17. H. S. Thayer, ed., *Newton's Philosophy of Nature* (New York: Hafner, 1953), 45.

18. Harrison Hayford, *Classic American Writers* (Boston: Little, Brown, 1962), 87.

19. Benjamin Franklin, *Benjamin Franklin's Autobiography* (New York: Rinehart, 1959), 292.

20. A. L. Rowse, *Shakespeare's Self-Portrait* (Lanham, Md.: University Press of America, 1985), 182.

21. William A. Eddy, *Satires and Personal Writings by Jonathan Swift* (London: Oxford University Press, 1932), 418.

22. Leo Tolstoy, *The Complete Works of Leo Tolstoy* (New York: Crowell, 1927), 378.

23. D. James Kennedy, *Why I Believe* (Dallas: Word, 1980), 40.

24. James Parton, *Life of Voltaire*, vol. 2 (Boston: Houghton Mifflin, 1884), 554.

25. Blaise Pascal, *Thoughts on Religion and Philosophy* (Edinburgh: Schultz), 5.

26. Michael Caputo, *God Seen Through the Eyes of the Great*

Minds (West Monroe, La.: Howard, 2000), 126.

27. Arthur H. Compton, *Chicago Daily News,* 12 April 1936.

28. A. Cressy Morrison, *Man Does Not Stand Alone* (Westwood, N.J.: Revell, 1944), 13.

29. John Ashton, *In Six Days* (Green Forest, Ark.: Master Books, 2000), 123.

30. Richard Swenson, *More Than Meets the Eye* (Colorado Springs: NavPress, 2000), 185.

31. Gerald Schroeder, *The Hidden Face of God* (New York: Simon & Schuster, 2001), 201.

32. Kitty Ferguson, *Stephen Hawking: Quest for a Theory of Everything* (New York: Bantam, 1992), 93.

33. Ashton, *In Six Days,* 155.

34. Ibid., 172.

35. Ibid., 271.

36. Lee Strobel, *The Case for Faith* (Grand Rapids, Mich.: Zondervan, 2000), 14.

37. Lewis, *Mere Christianity,* 48–49.

Max Davis, MA, is a husband and father of three. In addition to holding degrees in journalism and theology, he has served as a pastor, UPS truck driver, and coach. He now devotes his time to writing and speaking.

Max enjoys hearing from his readers. Receiving letters is a source of encouragement for him. He saves every letter and attempts to personally respond to each one. He can be persuaded to leave home to speak at conferences, retreats, and churches. To contact Max, write to:

Max Davis
22083 Greenwell Springs Rd
Greenwell Springs, LA 70739

Or e-mail at: mdbook@aol.com

The Word at Work . . .

What would you do if you wanted to share God's love with children on the streets of your city? That's the dilemma David C. Cook faced in 1870s Chicago. His answer was to create literature that would capture children's hearts.

Out of those humble beginnings grew a worldwide ministry that has used literature to proclaim God's love and disciple generation after generation. Cook Communications Ministries is committed to personal discipleship—to helping people of all ages learn God's Word, embrace his salvation, walk in his ways, and minister in his name.

Opportunities—and Crisis

We live in a land of plenty—including plenty of Christian literature! But what about the rest of the world? Jesus commanded, "Go and make disciples of all nations" (Matt. 28:19) and we want to obey this commandment. But how does a publishing organization "go" into all the world?

There are five times as many Christians around the world as there are in North America. Christian workers in many of these countries have no more than a New Testament, or perhaps a single shared copy of the Bible, from which to learn and teach.

We are committed to sharing what God has given us with such Christians.

A vital part of Cook Communications Ministries is our international out-reach, Cook Communications Ministries International (CCMI). Your pur-chase of this book, and of other books and Christian-growth products from Cook, enables CCMI to provide Bibles and Christian literature to people in more than 150 languages in 65 countries.

Cook Communications Ministries is a not-for-profit, self-supporting organization. Revenues from sales of our books, Bible curriculum, and other church and home products not only fund our U.S. ministry, but also fund our CCMI ministry around the world. One hundred percent of donations to CCMI go to our international literature programs.

... Around the World

CCMI reaches out internationally in three ways:

· Our premier International Christian Publishing Institute (ICPI) trains leaders from nationally led publishing houses around the world to develop evangelism and discipleship materials to transform lives in their countries.

· We provide literature for pastors, evangelists, and Christian workers in their national language. We provide study helps for pastors and lay leaders in many parts of the world, such as China, India, Cuba, Iran, and Vietnam.

· We reach people at risk—refugees, AIDS victims, street children, and famine victims—with God's Word. CCMI puts literature that shares the Good News into the hands of people at spiritual risk—people who might die before they hear the name of Jesus and are transformed by his love.

Word Power—God's Power

Faith Kidz, RiverOak, Honor, Life Journey, Victor, NexGen — every time you purchase a book produced by Cook Communications Ministries, you not only meet a vital personal need in your life or in the life of someone you love, but you're also a part of ministering to José in Colombia, Humberto in Chile, Gousa in India, or Lidiane in Brazil. You help make it possible for a pastor in China, a child in Peru, or a mother in West Africa to enjoy a life-changing book. And because you helped, children and adults around the world are learning God's Word and walking in his ways.

Thank you for your partnership in helping to disciple the world. May God bless you with the power of his Word in your life.

For more information about our international ministries, visit www.ccmi.org.